Talking Business:
Making Communication Work

Talking Business: Making Communication Work

David Clutterbuck and Sheila Hirst

Researched by Stephanie Cage

OXFORD   AMSTERDAM   BOSTON   LONDON   NEW YORK   PARIS
SAN DIEGO   SAN FRANCISCO   SINGAPORE   SYDNEY   TOKYO

Butterworth-Heinemann
An imprint of Elsevier Science
Linacre House, Jordan Hill, Oxford OX2 8DP
200 Wheeler Road, Burlington, MA 01803

First published 2003

British Library Cataloguing in Publication Data
A catalogue record for this book is available from the British Library

Library of Congress Cataloguing in Publication Data
A catalogue record for this book is available from the Library of Congress

ISBN 0 7506 5499 6

For information on all Butterworth-Heinemann publications visit our
website at: www.bh.com

Composition by Genesis Typesetting, Rochester, Kent
Printed and bound in Great Britain by Biddles Ltd, *www.biddles.co.uk*

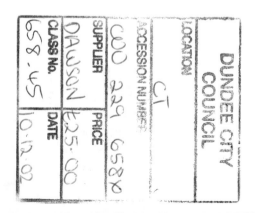

Contents

Figures

Tables

Acknowledgements

We would like to thank everyone at **item** who contributed to this book, especially Clive, Alison, Karen, Domna and Cami for their valuable input, Ian and Anthony for their assistance with the case studies, Debs and John for making the visuals happen, and Matt for helping put it all together.

We would also like to thank Susan Walker at MORI for providing us with some useful facts and figures.

Our thanks go to all at Butterworth-Heinemann for making this book possible. Lastly, but perhaps most importantly, thanks to all the organizations featured in the book for their time and generosity in sharing their experiences.

Preface

Why do we need another book about communication? It does not take much of a search through the many publications on internal (employee) communication, to realize that almost everything available is either focused on telling people how to make better presentations/influence people, or is heavily biased towards the academic.

The problem with the former is that printed advice is one of the least effective means of bringing about personal change. Moreover, for the communication professional or the manager, whose need concerns achieving effective organizational communication, there is little in these publications to make their job easier: a job increasingly dominated by the need to support and encourage major change within their organization.

The problem with academic texts is that they tend to be very narrowly focused on a specific issue, which may or not be relevant to practical application. The academic search for truth is neither interested in, nor intended to address, what is keeping managers awake at night.

There are surprisingly few resources of comprehensive guidance for those entrusted with making communication work in organizations. (We use throughout this book the term *communication* for the process and skill of communicating; *communications* for the technologies that enable communicating.) At the level of implementation, *The Gower Handbook of Employee Communication*, which we created in 1997, remains a primary source of reference, particularly in the UK and Europe. Now, in this volume, we aim to fill some of the gap in relating communication strategy both to the business priorities and to the implementation processes.

This book is not intended to give detailed step-by-step instructions on every piece of successful practice. It is intended to provide a clear route map for those struggling with the challenge of making their organization's employee communications equal to the task.

In short, we offer you in *Talking Business* a whirlwind tour through today's and tomorrow's world of internal communication. We guarantee that you will find some new ideas, some new ways of tackling employee communication issues, some new arguments for achieving communication objectives. Please sit back comfortably and enjoy the ride.

David Clutterbuck and Sheila Hirst
May 2002

Abbreviations

AI	artificial intelligence
ASPIC	Association for Strategy and Planning in Internal Communication
CEO	chief executive officer
CIPD	Chartered Institute of Personnel and Development
CIR	critical incident reporting
CRM	customer relationship management
DfEE	Department for Education and Employment
DTI	Department of Trade and Industry
ERM	employee relationship management
GICS	Government Information and Communication Services
HR	Human Resources
IABC	International Association of Business Communicators
IC	internal communication
IRM	investor relationship management
IT	information technology
M&A	mergers and acquisitions
PR	public relations
PRS	personal reflective space
SPEX	Shell Philippines Exploration

Introduction

What is the need for internal communication?

One of the depressing features of MORI surveys of internal communication is how little impact much of the activity in this area appears to have made. Over a period of thirty years, employees' average satisfaction with communications from their organization has remained steady at around 50 per cent.

Yet internal communication activity has blossomed in recent years. According to **item** research, the number of people employed inside companies in internal communication roles has risen steadily in the past decade, with under a fifth of communication departments boasting five or more full time professionals in 1996, compared with almost a third in 2001. The scope of their activities has also increased, with the majority of communicators saying they feel their role is more strategic, more clearly defined and more valued than five years ago. The function now attracts some of the brightest of the rising stars in organizations.

In their responses to questions raised in the Business Intelligence reports of 1996 and 2001, the heads of internal communication functions admit, too, that those areas of activity, which they recognize as having greatest value for the business are all too often those that they deliver on least effectively. Roles which communications professionals consider among the most important but least successful are improving managers' communication skills, enhancing employees' motivation, communicating the company's mission, vision and values, enhancing the credibility of the top team and encouraging feedback.

So what has gone wrong? Is it just that internal communication, like any other business discipline, is going through a natural maturing process, under which enthusiasm gradually becomes replaced by efficacy? Or are there serious flaws in the concept and practice of employee communication?

The answer, we believe, lies somewhere in between the two. Part of the problem is that people's expectations have increased alongside organizations' capacity to deliver. A rough estimate is that the volume of information readily available to people in the developed world – both at work and at home – has doubled every five years over the past three decades. (The actual volume of information generated has almost certainly increased even faster, but the capacity to access it easily has lagged behind.)

The explosion of web sites and databases is only part of the picture. The number of print-based periodicals on retailers' shelves has also expanded dramatically. The UK Periodical Publisher's Association registers about 3000 titles, while the European Federation of Magazine Publishers represents 36 000. In 2000, the US-based National Directory of Magazines listed about 17 800 publications (up from 14 000 in 1990). In a world where information on all manner of topics – from medicine to macramé, politics to pornography – is on open access, it is hardly surprising that people expect a similar level of disclosure at work.

However, communication is not just about making information available. That is the easy bit and the main contribution of e-technology has been to increase the emphasis organizations place on one-way communication. To feel that they are in genuine communication people require an interaction. No matter how personalized a one-way communication is, it cannot provide the intellectual and emotional engagement that comes from discussion and, at a higher level of interaction, from dialogue. When people complain that they do not feel the organization or their managers communicate well with them, they typically are concerned less about raw information than the quality of the interactions that give them context and a sense of involvement. Yet, wherever we look in large organizations, we see that the bulk of communication spend is on media, which are predominantly one-way in their application and impact.

In terms of stimulating genuine, lasting change, we can categorize communication as shown in Table 1.

Common myths about communication in organizations

Most people in organizations still operate under a series of misconceptions about the nature of communication. This hampers them using communication as an effective driver of strategic change. This book aims, in part, to address the misconceptions and to suggest practical alternative concepts and approaches – in some cases backed up by examples from the experience of companies which have attempted to take a more strategic view

Table 1 Communication style versus impact

Style	Type of media	Type and scale of impact
Informing	Memoranda, employee periodicals (print and e-zine), most intranet sites	Raising awareness Change index* = 1
Discussion	Briefing groups, chat rooms	Raising understanding Change index* = 3
Dialogue	Facilitated meetings, coaching and mentoring sessions, team learning	Building commitment and stimulating behaviour change Change index* = 8–10

Note: *item's change index is a measure of the potential to bring about major positive changes for the organization.

of communication. (Please note that we use 'strategic' here in a very specific manner – to mean the close alignment of the communication process with clear business goals and priorities.)

Among these myths of organizational communication are:

- *Communication is something you do to people.* Top management in many companies perceive communication as a process of getting messages across to the employees, so that they know what is expected of them and why. Effective communication, however, is a process of dialogue, which we can define as *the development of mutual understanding*. Cases such as BP's diversity programme illustrate how much more powerful dialogue can be than instruction or discussion.
- *Most managers are reasonably good communicators, otherwise they would not be in the role.* This is like saying that being a good parent comes naturally. To a few, fortunate people, it does. Most of us are passable at parenting and at communicating – we do the best we can – and some are just plain dreadful. The reality in most organizations is that most managers spend a high proportion of their time *avoiding* communicating. When it is done well it demands substantial mental effort, the allocation of reflective time and the courage to face up to challenge and/ or discomfort.
- *You are either a good communicator or you are not.* Again, our research shows that this view (paradoxically often held simultaneously with the previous) is simplistic and largely

inaccurate. Yes, there are people with specific communication defects – for example, those who suffer from forms of Asperger Syndrome or Semantic Pragmatic Disorder – but for most people, communication competence is a *situational* skill. You may have an employee, who appears to be very poor at listening. Start talking about his or her next salary increase, or favourite football club, and that employee is likely to transform into a remarkably attentive listener.

- *Communication is the job of the communication function.* This is akin to saying that Human Resources (HR) is the responsibility of the HR function. In both cases, the function is no more than being a co-ordinator and enabler – the provider of support systems and advice to managers on how to contribute. The more a company tries to shift the responsibility for communication onto the communication professionals, the less communication actually takes place.

- *Awards and prizes by external bodies are a demonstration and recognition of communication excellence.* Wrong! Our researches show that there is little or no correlation between these two factors. On the contrary: professionally produced, prize-winning employee periodicals or web sites are very frequently associated with poor business performance (along with the flagpole, fishpond and corporate jet!). Only when media contribute significantly to the achievement of business goals and priorities do they add value.

- *Communication can (or should) be controlled.* The reality is that probably less than 10 per cent of communication in an organization is formal. The rest happens through informal exchanges at coffee machines, by e-mail and through more subtle media, such as behaviour and what is *not* said. Of that 10 per cent, the vast majority comes through a mixture of staff and line, with the communication function generating no more than 2 per cent. Human Resources, operations, legal, information technology (IT) and other functions are constantly engaged in communicating (or some semblance of it). The communication function that attempts to control communication simply generates new forms of informal channel. A more effective role for the function is to enable communication and help raise its quality in terms of relevance, reliability and clarity.

- *There is/should be a clear chain of communication, alongside the chain of command.* Given the increasingly rapid spread of matrix structures in organizations – often with more than two dimensions – it is very difficult to see how this could apply in such an environment. Even in a more traditional structure, however, the flow of communication is broadly chaotic and

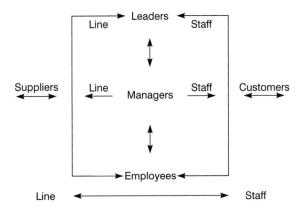

this phenomenon has been reinforced by the ability of e-mail to cut across departmental and hierarchical barriers. The diagram illustrates the different links in the communication chain. Gaps commonly appear in all or some of them depending on the organization.

All these issues are addressed in greater depth in the chapters of this book, which draws together theory, research, practical experience and pragmatic advice.

Why do businesses need to communicate better?

From Peter Drucker to Tom Peters and current management gurus, there have been two consistent strains – the importance of leadership behaviour and the value of communication as the glue that holds the organization together. Numerous studies of senior management attitudes confirm the same picture – communication matters. One MORI survey of board directors and other influential business people found that 76 per cent believed that cultivating goodwill among existing employees is essential. In fact, employees came second to only one other stakeholder group – existing customers, at 80 per cent.

Where the evidence is sadly lacking is for the importance of the internal communication function. In **item**'s research for the International Association of Business Communicators (IABC) study into the relationship between communication competence and business success, we examined over a hundred research reports, papers and articles and found at best partial support for the view that the internal communication (IC) function did anything demonstrably useful.

So why has the IC function grown so rapidly? Some of the key factors include:

1 Desperation by top management to make strategy happen. In flatter hierarchies, it becomes much more important for people to understand what they are supposed to do and why. There are fewer people to point them in the right direction – most knowledge/service workers are to a greater or lesser extent on their own.
2 The speed of change means that top management has to sustain people's interest and commitment, overcoming their resistance to initiatives.
3 Increasing mergers and acquisition (M&A) activity creates new anxieties, which must be managed if the new company is not to be mired in recriminations.
4 Fear by top management about losing control of communication, as technology allows people access to almost anything and encourages people to communicate directly rather than through hierarchical silos. E-technology increases their sense of anxiety, as more and more people feel besieged by information rather than liberated by it.
5 Increasing attention to brand and corporate reputation means that companies need consistency in what people say and do, at all levels.
6 Retaining people is the big challenge for knowledge businesses – being informed is one of the ways to help keep them.
7 Other functions within the business need help with their own internal reputation. Most professionals do not see marketing as part of their own role, and even if they have the skills, many find it difficult to make time for it, so they have begun to turn to IC for help.

All these pressures have helped raise top management's expectation of IC from being a small-time provider of services (company periodical, some speechwriting for the chief executive officer and organizing the occasional event) to an advisory function, a little like HR in that it helps them to avoid problems. There is now a gradual evolution, to an internal consultancy, which enables the business to use communication for competitive advantage – that's the challenge to IC for the *next* decade.

A bedrock theory of employee communication

Because everyone communicates (we now finally even appear to know the specific gene sets that give humans this special capability), people tend to assume that they have a common understanding of what communication is, what it is for and how it works. Even communication professionals often take these same assumptions for granted, although they should be at least peripherally aware that those who come from, say, a marketing background are likely to have different perceptions of communication from those with an Human Resources background. (This simple sentence illustrates the point – why do we feel obliged to capitalize HR, but not marketing?)

So before we get too deeply into the nitty-gritty of communication strategy, let us consider for a moment what we mean by communication and by employee communication.

The nature of communication

Communication occurs whenever there is a meaningful interchange between two or more people. You might be tempted to insert the words 'of information' in that terse definition, but there are at least two good reasons not to. One is that a great deal of communication occurs at the unconscious sensory level. This is not strictly information, but data. Data only becomes information when it is structured to elicit some form of meaning. The second is that, in addition to the transfer of data and information, communication may also transfer knowledge (information structured in a way that makes it useful for making choices or decisions); skills (knowledge and information translated into practical application or know-how); and wisdom (the ability to extrapolate from data, information, knowledge and skills to tackle new situations).

Key to effective communication, whether between individuals, organizations or a combination of the two, is structure. The

Table 2 The cascade of communication

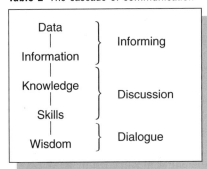

essence of language is a shared set of norms about meaning and about the order in which elements of meaning are transmitted. In general, linguistic psychologists such as Steven Pinker (author of *The Language Instinct*, 1994) believe that most of these rules are genetically imprinted. Structure reduces the mental effort in analysing communication, because the rules largely predict the meaning. Wordplays amuse, because they retain expected structures, while changing the expected meaning.

Although some purposes of communication (for example, international conventions or treaties) may be best served by encouraging multiple interpretations of the same text, in general, greater clarity of meaning – where everyone has a similar understanding of what is meant – is normally beneficial on all sides. However, clarity is often low because:

- people place different filters, based on culture, personality or experience, on what they hear
- people often speak before they have sorted out in their mind *what they want to say* and *what impact they want it to have* (then they are surprised by the other person's reaction!)
- people are reluctant to cause themselves or others pain or embarrassment by pointing out directly things that they think are wrong
- people do not recognize their own or other people's stereotypes
- people often lack the verbal dexterity to express ideas concisely and accurately, or in language appropriate to the recipients
- good communication requires an appropriate balance of intellectual observation/analysis and emotional involvement. When the balance is disturbed, in either direction, communication is disrupted
- when there are too many ideas to be communicated at the same time, either the speaker or the receiver (or both) is likely to suffer from 'channel overload'.

These seven causes of low clarity in communication apply equally to individuals and to organizations. In both cases, considerable improvements can be made by a planned approach that helps the individual or organization to address each factor as a development issue. Developing the competence of dialogue requires changes in both behaviour and process.

For the moment, however, let us focus on the organizational issues. Given that clarity is so important, one of the first tasks of any internal communication department is to define what internal communication is.

The purpose of internal communication

This is the point where it is tempting to embark on a lengthy discussion of the merits of different definitions. Our experience, however, is that this does little to clarify, and may even make meaning more obscure. So we unashamedly assert that:

> The purpose of internal communication is to assist people in an organization to work together and learn together in pursuit of shared goals and/or the mutual creation of value.

Let us take the key elements of this one by one. The purpose is *to assist people* because effective communication is a collaborative process, which relies on their willingness to share information and to listen to others. People need communication *to work together*, i.e. to link their activities with those of others in the organization, and with people outside the organization, such as customers and suppliers. They also need to *learn together* to adapt what they and the organization do to changes in their environment.

Pursuing *shared goals* does not mean that everyone has to share exactly the same goals. There has to be at least one broad, differentiating goal that everyone signs up to – like staying in business by building customer loyalty – but subgoals may be different between working groups. People's individual goals also need to be recognized, accepted as valid, and accommodated to a level which seems reasonable to them, the organization and other stakeholders, inside or outside the organization.

The same is true of *mutual creation of value*. The concept is best expressed in the diagram.

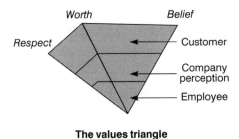

The values triangle

Basically, the more the organization and the people in it focus on

- building value (in the sense of worth of shares for investors, marketability for employees etc.)
- demonstrating value (in the sense of showing that you respect and appreciate each other's efforts and contributions)

- understanding values (in the sense of what people believe, what is important to them),

the more likely the organization is to achieve the state of *continuous constructive dialogue*, which should be the foundation of innovation, teamwork and all those other enabling behaviours that lead to sustainable competitive advantage.

In essence, communication is a contract between individuals, the organization and each other. Communication only works when people are willing to engage with others. The *quality* of communication depends on whether the 'contract' is one of listening, discussing or genuine dialogue.

Improving the quality of communication takes time and sustained energy. It can be useful to think of the journey as one towards *communication maturity*, which is in effect *the ability of individuals and the organization to engage in continuous dialogue that leads to action.* This concept is explored further in Chapter 6, 'Communicating during radical change'.

The role of the internal communication function

Based on the definition of purpose for internal communication, the IC function can be defined as *to support and enable the communication process within the organization.*

We can further refine that bald statement to say that the role is primarily:

To assist the organization and the people within it to enhance communication capability and

To provide support, in the form of advice, measurement processes and practical help in the design and delivery of media.

This is a very broad remit, which covers almost any area of activity within an organization. It is not surprising that many companies place young high-flyers in the internal communication function, recognizing that they will have here an opportunity to get to know the company very widely, develop an extensive network of senior management contacts and insights into how the systems really work.

Just how wide the remit is, is illustrated by the involvement of the internal communication function.

The very breadth of activity is also a problem, however. Many IC departments we have spoken to at Association for Strategy and Planning in Internal Communication (ASPIC) events and in

Table 3 Involvement of the internal communication function

	Delivery	Advisory
Strategic	Communication planning	Internal consultancy
Tactical	Media (e.g. employee newspapers, intranet content); events	Communication coaching

our research for *Transforming Internal Communication* (Kernaghan, Clutterbuck and Cage, 2001) state that they are concerned that their ability to offer strategic services is constrained by the fact that senior managers associate their skills more closely with tactical delivery. This is a problem shared by, for example, IT and HR, both of which are now commonly resolving the dilemma by outsourcing the tactical delivery activities entirely. Within internal communication, there is little outsourcing as yet. A third of communication departments we studied for *Transforming Internal Communication* do not outsource any work, and over half outsource less than a quarter of their communication. Although outsourcing is as yet generally on an ad hoc basis, rather than part of a planned positioning of the function towards its internal customers, about two-fifths of survey respondents expected the amount of outsourcing in their organization to increase, compared with only a tenth who expected it to decrease.

The core constituents of the internal communication process

Wherever and however the internal communication function intervenes to fulfil these roles, it requires a robust process. Although the specific requirement and circumstances of communication will vary widely, all interventions are enhanced by adherence to the process in the diagram on the following page.

Signposts and structure of what follows

In the chapters that follow, we will expand upon all these concepts, exploring current thinking and good practice around internal communication.

Chapter 1 discusses the link between business performance and what the internal communication function does. The core of this chapter is a ground-breaking study, carried out by **item** for the

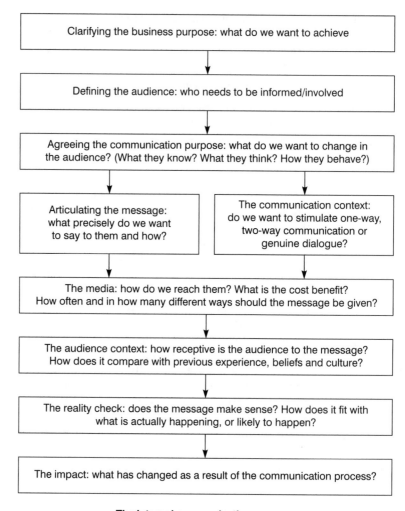

Clarifying the business purpose: what do we want to achieve

Defining the audience: who needs to be informed/involved

Agreeing the communication purpose: what do we want to change in the audience? (What they know? What they think? How they behave?)

Articulating the message: what precisely do we want to say to them and how?

The communication context: do we want to stimulate one-way, two-way communication or genuine dialogue?

The media: how do we reach them? What is the cost benefit? How often and in how many different ways should the message be given?

The audience context: how receptive is the audience to the message? How does it compare with previous experience, beliefs and culture?

The reality check: does the message make sense? How does it fit with what is actually happening, or likely to happen?

The impact: what has changed as a result of the communication process?

The internal communication process

IABC. The study involved a group of companies operating internationally, ranging in business performance from very strong to fairly weak. Within the group, we compared the key competencies of an internal communications function as defined by a massive literature search and the perceptions of focus groups of communication professionals. The competencies comprised:

- strategic communication planning
- effective management of communication activity
- experience, capability and skills of communication professionals
- high-quality communication media and tools.

It emerged that there was *no* correlation between the excellence of the IC function in any of these areas and that of the business at either the macro level (financial performance) or the micro level (successful delivery of major change programmes). However, a very strong correlation did emerge between business success and four key aspects of communication:

- clarity of purpose
- effective interfaces
- effective information sharing
- communication behaviour of leaders.

It seems that the internal communication function adds greatest value to the business when its activities are focused on supporting these aspects of communication. Winning awards for deliverables may be great for the ego, but may not be particularly useful for the business!

Chapter 2 describes some core concepts relevant to the understanding of internal communication, such as the idea of receptivity to communication, the principles of measuring communication success and the importance of dialogue. We also look briefly at the internal communication function's role as an *enabler* as opposed to a deliverer.

Chapter 3 examines the business case for internal communication in more detail and looks at how communication actually happens in organizations. The proportion of communication that is under the control of the internal communication function is very small – typically less than 2 per cent. So how can a small department affect the quality of communication more widely? Every other function in the business needs to communicate, but how does it learn to do so more effectively, and how can the IC function help? Evidence from other functions, such as HR, suggests strongly that the ability to influence the organization positively is closely linked to how they provide proactive support to other areas of the business. We examine how to build and maintain such partnerships and provide practical processes for linking communication effort to business priorities at both the business and functional strategy levels.

Chapter 4 expands the context beyond the boundaries of the organization and examines the interfaces between internal and external audiences. It is increasingly clear that a message to one stakeholder audience quickly spreads to others. One large retailer made the mistake, not long ago, of putting a different spin on its messages to employees than that in its annual report to shareholders. It forgot that loyal employees might belong to both audiences. The fallout damaged its relationships with both groups of stakeholders. We present some practical ways of analysing stakeholder interactions.

We also develop the argument that stakeholder management begins with employee communication and that making employees ambassadors for the business should be a priority for every organization. Along the way, we also explore how to build trust between the company and its stakeholders, again beginning with the employees.

Chapter 5 looks at communicating the corporate vision and values. The extent, to which employees can be motivated by abstract goals originating in executive suites, or by aspirational values, is much lower than leaders often think. Rather than respond cynically, however, the organization can achieve much by taking a more bottom-up approach that begins with 'What kind of company would we like to work for?' and focuses communication effort on how the leaders and followers together can achieve that.

Chapter 6 is the first of several chapters dealing with issues related to change. The core issue here is: how do you use communication processes to change people's beliefs, attitudes and behaviours? And to what extent is it ethical to do so?

We also explore the issues of cultural diversity and how positive dialogue can enhance the respect and value placed upon different views and cultural backgrounds. Chapter 6 also takes a brief look at the challenges involved in changing the culture, and the difficulties of communicating across a variety of cultures, both corporate and national.

In many cases, cultural change is initiated by the need to align employees behind a set of brand values. Chapter 7 examines the four different expressions of a company's brand – corporate, product, employer and employee – and how they can be made to support each other, with the help of effective communication processes. Integrating the four brand expressions is critical in presenting a coherent organizational personality to both internal and external audiences.

Chapter 8 rounds off the section on change. Merger and acquisition are often among the most drastic upheavals employees encounter and there is an obvious and substantial need for constant, credible communication throughout the process. We look to good practice around the world to provide a pragmatic template for addressing the communication process, starting before the public announcement and for a year or more thereafter.

In Chapter 9, we examine communication capability from the perspective of interpersonal competence. From a brief overview of the psychology of communication, we present the concept of *situational communication* – the recognition that communication competence depends heavily on the context, in which the interaction occurs. Although many companies assess managers on communication competence as part of their regular perform-ance appraisal, they tend to do so without reference to context. Moreover, the range of skills assessed is usually limited to presentation and listening. We show how this approach under-mines people's confidence and often *prevents* them putting committed effort into developing their communication capability.

Much has also been made of communication style. We question the basis of diagnostics that assume communication style is simply a reflection of personality and offer an alternative perspective.

Chapter 10 deals with how to build communication capability through attention to new technologies, i.e from a process perspective. We also assess the potential of the electronic technologies to enhance communication and how to overcome some of the most serious barriers. What role has the IC function in helping people deal with information overload, for example?

Perhaps the greatest problem of all, however, in this context is the rapid reduction in face-to-face communication in favour of e-mail. While there are many benefits from having fewer meetings, the evidence is strong that dispersed teams – especially when they involve people from different cultural backgrounds – are less effective than teams that meet regularly. How can the IC function help organizations restore the balance between transac-tional and relationship-building communication?

Finally, in Chapter 11, we discuss how to consolidate commu-nication capability into the instinctive systems and infrastructure of the business, so that it genuinely does become a source of strategic advantage. We ask what tomorrow's *World Class Communicating Company* will look like, provide some answers and suggest practical steps for building just such an organization.

References

Kernaghan, S., Clutterbuck, D. and Cage, S. (2001). *Transforming Internal Communication*. Business Intelligence.

Pinker, S. (1994). *The Language Instinct*. Morrow.

1

Business performance and communication excellence

This chapter could equally have been titled 'The business case for employee communication'. Before we can embark upon a rational discussion of the strategic role of employee communication in a business, we must first illuminate the link between the two issues. In other words, how do we know that employee communication can or does have an impact on the business at all?

Until recently, the contention that there is a link has been largely an act of faith. Numerous management gurus refer to the importance of communication in achieving strategic objectives, but offer little in the way of evidence, or even an explanation of the contributory mechanisms.

Jack Welch is quoted in *Control your Destiny or Someone Else Will* (Tichy and Sherman, 1993) as saying:

> If you want to get the benefit of everything employees have, you've got to free them, make everybody a participant. Everybody has to know everything, so they can make the right decisions by themselves ... The role of the leader is to express a vision, get buy-in and implement it. That calls for open, caring relations with every employee, and face-to-face communication.

This view undoubtedly accounts for much of Welch's success and popularity as a business leader, but still fails to take account of the many practical obstacles to openness which managers face every day, from time constraints to regulatory issues.

Peters and Waterman (1982) concluded in *In Search of Excellence* that 'excellent companies are a vast network of informal, open communications'. Communication was clearly one of the areas contributing to business success, but the authors found difficulty in conveying the elements of successful communication, let alone showing how to achieve success in this area. The difficulty of altering behaviours to achieve successful communication is compounded by the fact that for most business leaders communication within the business is not the area of activity they most enjoy – far from it. They are typically motivated by the next deal, by innovation, by hands-on involvement in the next big project. While this may require some time on communication, it requires a clear connection between the goal they have set and the communication process for them to become both emotionally and intellectually hooked into communication as a priority activity.

It is relatively easy for Human Resources to explain that 'If you don't invest X amount in raising salaries for first line supervisors, there will be an increase of Y in turnover amongst that group. That will cost you Z and you won't be able to push through the change programme you have invested so much energy in'. Similarly, the IT function can draw a chain of connection between investment in new resources, speed and accuracy of response to customer enquiries, and the proportion of enquiries that result in orders.

In each of these cases there is a clear chain of cause and effect, the possibility of measuring the impact of investment and a relatively clear decision to make: invest and the advantage is this; do not invest and the likely penalty will be that. For employee communication, it is much harder to establish that chain. Until recently, the nearest model was the service-profit chain (Loveman et al., 1994), which aims to demonstrate the causal links between employee satisfaction, customer satisfaction, customer loyalty and business profitability. The model, developed by Harvard Business School faculty team Loveman, Heskett, Jones, Schlesinger and Sasser, shows how employee satisfaction leads to improved retention, which in turn results in better external service, better customer satisfaction, improved customer retention and, ultimately, higher profits.

Although widely regarded as a sound theoretical model, the connections in the service-profit chain model have generally not been proven. Like quantum theory, it is a good enough model

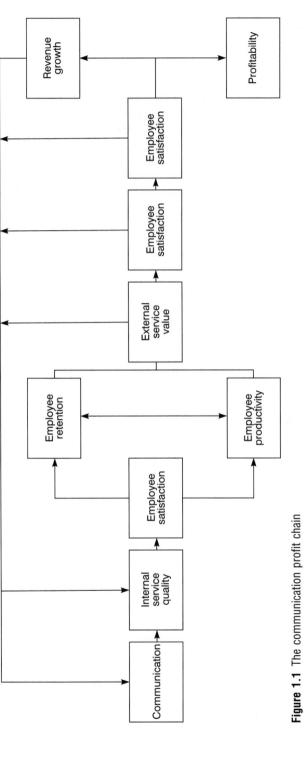

Figure 1.1 The communication profit chain

until a better one comes along. But communication is only a small element in the model and all too easily dismissed as insignificant within the grand picture.

A model, which placed more emphasis on employee communication, would look like the one shown in Figure 1.1.

One potential weakness with this approach is that leadership communication is typically seen as a top-down approach, yet communication within modern organizations consists mainly of interchanges between peers. Classic models of communication such as Likert's (1961) linking pin model assumed a command and tell, hierarchical organizational structure, which is no longer typical. Hence the inclusion in the communication profit chain model of employee empowerment as a counterbalance that places more emphasis on discussion and dialogue than on instruction.

On its own, however, while the communication profit chain may convince top management intellectually, it is unlikely to seize their emotional commitment. There are just too many links in the chain to be convincing from a personal effort–reward perspective. More direct evidence is needed to persuade executives to make personal changes in priorities and behaviours.

Over the past decade or so, several organizations with a vested interest in communication and a number of academics have attempted to demonstrate this more direct link. Companies such as Bass Taverns and BP Chemicals in the UK have credited communication programmes with a major part of their success. Sears Roebuck, in the USA, has demonstrated (using the service-profit chain model) the connection between employee satisfaction and business success, but stopped short of showing the specific contribution of communication to employee satisfaction.

Some more general studies have explored the impact of communication across a number of companies. The UK report, *Tomorrow's Company* produced by the Royal Society of Arts in 1995, concluded that the successful company of the future would 'actively communicate with and involve a wide range of stakeholder groups, not just shareholders'. Another UK report *Partnership with People*, produced in conjunction with the department of Trade and Industry (DTI), the Department for Education and Employment (DfEE), the University of Brighton and the Chartered Institute of Personnel and Development (CIPD), claimed that communication is considered a key means of ensuring people's motivation and involvement in the business, and that this has become a high priority over the last few years, but did not provide any substantive evidence in support of the popularity of this view.

In summary, these various studies all help to build the big picture, but they are not convincing, often contradictory and still do not provide a comprehensive model of how employee communication impacts business results. Back to square one!

Cracking the code

In 1998, the IABC, based in California, decided it wanted to break this impasse. It conducted an international competition for proposals on how to establish the link. The competition was won by **item**, partly because of the rigour of the approach suggested, but also because of our previous experience in designing and conducting studies of business excellence (Goldsmith and Clutterbuck, 1984; 1998).

The approach we adopted involved four main steps: developing a viable measure of business performance, developing a measure of communication excellence, gathering data by using these measures on a sample of multinational companies and analysing the data to draw conclusions about the links, if any, between communication activity and business success.

In all the studies of business excellence that have been carried out since the early 1980s, one of the basic assumptions has been that simply measuring a company by its reported performance in the annual report is not an adequate guide. Not only is the annual report just a snapshot in time, but it provides only a one-dimensional (financial) measure. Differences in financial reporting methods also make it problematic to compare businesses based in one country with those in another. Moreover, an increasing number of businesses do not measure themselves solely on financial criteria. Body Shop, Patagonia and Ben and Jerry's, for example, have a mixture of financial and social objectives to pursue.

Other critical indicators of excellence include organic growth in market share, reputation among peer companies, general public reputation and the quality of leadership, as assessed by the investment community. Add to this an element of what the company itself perceives success to be and there emerges a kind of balanced scorecard, which more accurately represents the overall performance of the business. (It is a bit like defining an individual as successful. We may say that someone is successful just because they have made a lot of money. But if they have had multiple divorces, have a reduced life expectancy through alcohol or drug abuse and have no time to enjoy their wealth, how successful are they? Success is a multifaceted diamond and to treat it in a one-dimensional manner is inadequate.)

Another problem in defining business success is accuracy of the measurements taken. To gather the data sufficient to assess each company on the balanced scorecard of success is both time-consuming and frustrating – not least, because the quality of data will vary considerably. When, in the early 1980s, the research team for *The Winning Streak* studies of high-performing UK companies set out to carry out this kind of analysis, it took several students many weeks to filter the Times 1000 companies down to fifty on the basis of their financial data, and as long again to extract half as many, which merited inclusion on a balanced scorecard basis.

One advantage we had for this study is that we did not want or need to identify just top performers. On the contrary, to make valid comparisons, we needed to start with a random collection of companies, ranging from high to low performers. This enabled us to take a new approach to the measurement process. First, we asked the companies to rate themselves on a scale of excellence in performance. Then we asked them to provide the documentary proof – financial reports, industry surveys, analysts reports, company reputation surveys and so on. Where the level of proof was not convincing, the company was asked to provide more or to reconsider its score, with the result that several were revised.

This process, which we believe to be unique in excellence studies, gave us a good variation of levels of business excellence. As an additional measure, we also asked each company to select one or two major communication projects, which we could examine on the basis of how well they fulfilled their business objectives.

The companies studied ranged in size from around 1000 employees worldwide to approaching 100 000. They included manufacturing, financial services, engineering, retail, IT and fast-moving consumer goods companies. There was a wide mix of cultures, although most of the organizations were UK-headquartered.

At the same time, we had to define what was meant by excellence in communication. Given the origins of the study, the focus of this element was the communication function. What characteristics compromised the key competencies for a communication function? (By communication function, we mean the management of communication processes across the organization, as opposed to communications, which refers to the technology supporting communication and is usually the responsibility of IT, telecommunications or other functions.)

Opinions about effective communication functions were not hard to come by. Indeed, the literature search involved several hundred papers, studies and articles. From these sources and

interviews with senior communication professionals, we identified a list of factors, which were subsequently refined into four
categories:

1 Having a *communication strategy*. (Although the experts and
   practitioners generally agreed this should be linked to business
   priorities, there was little agreement about how to do so.)
2 Effective *management processes* to implement the plan.
3 Experienced and capable *communication professionals*.
4 High-quality *communication media and tools*.

To assess the quality of each of these factors in each organization
and for each of the projects identified, we interviewed the
communication professionals and a variety of managers and
other employees. This gave us the data to assign a numerical
value to each of the four factors, in each company.

What we hoped to find was a straight-line correlation between
excellence in business performance and these communication
activities. The reality was very different, as Figure 1.2 indicates.
On all four factors there was no discernible pattern of positive
connection between what the communication function did and
either the performance of the business or the delivery and
contribution to the business of key business projects. Some of the
most successful projects had very little input from communication professionals, being run by line managers; others, where the
communication team was strongly involved, had very dis-
appointing results.

One of the great benefits of qualitative studies is that, if the

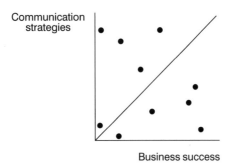

Figure 1.2 What we found

initial hypothesis turns out to be untenable, it is possible to mine
the data to find and test alternative hypotheses. So we reviewed
the interviews for clues to other factors, which might show a
higher correlation.

Very soon, it became clear that, while the notion of the communication function having a *direct* influence on the success factors of the business was not upheld by our results, there were clear indicators of *indirect* impact. It seems that the function is able to contribute best to the organization when it is working to support four *organizational* competencies:

- clarity of purpose – where the business (or project) has a very clear set of goals and priorities, understood by everyone; and where people are able to relate their own activities directly to the achievement of those goals (Figure 1.3)
- trusting interfaces between people at all levels between leaders and the employees; managers and their direct reports; employees with each other, along the supply chains and in working teams; and between the business and its customers and suppliers
- effective sharing of information – where systems and networks enable people to have the right information at the right time to do their job; share opinions and discuss ideas; circulate best practice; and learn from each other (Figure 1.4)

Figure 1.3 The evidence: how clarity of purpose relates to business success

Figure 1.4 The evidence: how effective interfaces relate to business success

- top management communication – when leaders' behaviour is consistent with what they are saying, both formally and informally and when they are seen as role models of good communication (Figure 1.5).

The correlation between performance in each of these activities or competencies and the success of the business or individual projects was remarkably high, as Figures 1.3, 1.4 and 1.5 indicate.

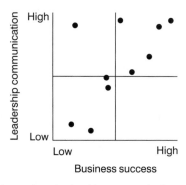

Figure 1.5 The evidence: how leadership communication relates to business success

In one case, the chief executive officer (CEO) was very active touring the sites, talking to people and demonstrating a commitment to communication and explaining his values. Yet people in the organization still had little sense of what the company was trying to achieve, and how it was going to beat the competition. Infighting between 'robber barons' in the divisions meant that there was no culture of trust, and outdated technology meant that knowledge and information sharing was patchy at best. This organization performed badly both overall as a business and in the implementation of individual projects. This case and others suggest that it is the combination of these four activities that counts. Being good at just one or two of them simply is not enough.

These four activities have been referred to as the four pillars of communication excellence and this is how we will refer to them in the rest of this book. Wherever the communication function used its professionalism and expertise in support of one or more of the pillars, there was a moderate to high level of success at both business and project levels (Figure 1.6).

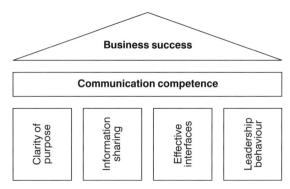

Figure 1.6 Four pillars of communication excellence

Implications of the four pillars of communication excellence

A number of companies have now used the four pillars as the basic building blocks upon which to restructure their communication function. Some have also established measurement processes, to track their success in each of those activities.

Indicators, which demonstrate clarity of purpose, for example, include:

- How understandable are the core messages on corporate direction?
- What proportion of employees at each level can explain the company's overall strategy?
- What proportion are able to discuss what that strategy means for their unit and their jobs?
- To what extent does top management 'sing from the same hymn sheet' when talking about the business and its competitive environment?
- How consistently are the business values reflected and reinforced in corporate publications?
- How clearly defined and communicated is the purpose behind each major change project?

Indicators for top management communication behaviour might include:

- How *credible* are members of the top team to other audiences within the company?
- Do employees feel they walk the talk (i.e. that their behaviour is consistent with what they demand of others)?

- Is communication an item on the board's agenda?
- Do the members of the top team demonstrate a real understanding of their responsibilities as leaders in communication?
- Do they exhibit a full portfolio of communication competencies – in particular, do they demonstrate good listening behaviours as well as presentation skills?
- Do employees believe that the top team is genuinely committed to open communication and dialogue?

For trusting relationships, some of the indicators are:

- Are people able to admit mistakes and weaknesses without fear of punishment and/or ridicule?
- Are different opinions and perspectives valued?
- Do employees believe top management cares about them and their concerns?
- Do people feel that their colleagues generally have goodwill towards them?
- Do people feel their colleagues are generally competent to do the job?
- Do they think top management is competent?
- Are messages from the centre accepted as accurate, or regarded with suspicion? (Do people mistrust corporate 'spin'?)
- Are people able to confront and discuss difficult issues openly? (i.e. is constructive criticism and challenge welcomed?)
- Are some minority groups sidelined and/or disenfranchised?

Finally, for effective information sharing:

- Do people know where and how to get the information they need to do their job well?
- Are people generous with their time and information towards others (individuals and teams)?
- Are there systems in place to make knowledge sharing easier?
- Are informal networks encouraged and supported?

If the scores are too low on one or more of the pillars, how can we remedy the issue(s)?

The four factors originally selected for evaluating communication functions can all be applied to very positive effect in supporting the four pillars. Strategic planning competence is essential in building and selling practical plans to bridge the gap between where the organization is now and where it intends to be. For example, achieving greater clarity of purpose may require a strategy to:

- gain top management sign up to the need for greater clarity
- help them establish genuine clarity and uniform understanding in their own minds as a precursor to doing the same for other people
- design and resource appropriate media to inform and educate people and to engage them in the kind of dialogue that enhances real understanding
- benchmark the communication differential with competitors (Are they getting their message across more effectively?)
- build frequent and consistent measurement to assess progress on clarity of purpose and to respond to any decline
- work with HR to recruit people likely to be 'online' with the business values before they join.

Following through the same example, effective management of the communication activity can help to ensure that, say, project management processes include time for reflection and review of decisions against the business and project purpose. Similarly, having well-constructed processes for managing major changes such as mergers or acquisitions also aids clarity of purpose because they should enable managers to lift their heads above the immediate, urgent priorities and check back against the big picture.

The professionalism of communication staff is one key to building trust and confidence among managers at all levels. It is important that they can seek and receive valuable and reliable advice about how and when to communicate key messages. By being proactive, warning managers when messages are likely to become confused and suggesting opportunities to reinforce them, the professional communicators enhance their own reputation and are able to maintain communication on the agenda.

High-quality media do not in themselves do much for the business. A shelf-full of trophies for design of periodicals or web sites may be good for the ego, but they are irrelevant unless they are earned by contributing to business goals. Take the simple example of an expensively designed and highly interactive web site detailing key suppliers. On the basis of hit rates, it was remarkably successful – except that the people accessing it were almost all employees making private purchases. The employees it was targeted at all had their own files with much the same (and more detailed) information.

Media that support clarity of purpose and the organization's business goals have very specific objectives about the audience they are aimed at and the messages and values they are intended to support. These themes are echoed frequently and the degree of impact (whether the audience recognizes, understands and/or acts upon the message) is measured constantly. They explain new thinking and important events – both external and internal to the organization – in the context of the business purpose. The strategic planning competence of the internal communication function can ensure that media are initiated and designed with these criteria and processes in mind. It can also ensure that the messages carried by different media are integrated into a thematic whole.

In the same way, each of the other three factors communication professionals identified as core to the function can be adapted to bring real focus to the communication activity. In some cases, this may mean a re-skilling of the professionals – for example, extending their understanding of business processes and building their skills of general management.

The core lesson, however, is that, like the finance function, most of the impact of the internal communication function comes not from what it does itself, but from what it enables and stimulates others to do. Moreover, the process of influencing people to communicate better is not a sole responsibility of the communication function; it is shared with top management, HR, IT and a number of other functions, as we shall explore in Chapter 3, 'The internal community of communication'. This may sound like a small change from the norm, but for most internal communication functions this is a major shift in attitude and one which they may initially have difficulty accepting and then selling to managers who have been quite comfortable in the illusion that communication is the communication department's problem.

Linking strategy and performance – all aboard?

Having a great strategy does not necessarily win wars, or market advantage. Less well-thought-through strategies, with less innovation, may easily deliver better performance if they are implemented more effectively. A reasonable conclusion from the **item** study is that aligning the communication processes more closely with the strategy will contribute significantly to the effectiveness of the implementation of the business strategy.

Take the example of differentiation through service. Clarity of purpose demands that the communication function help ensure that everyone in the business, whether customer-facing or not, recognizes why service issues are important, what the impact of service failure is, and what they can do about it in their daily routine. Improving the quality of interfaces might mean helping teams understand the difficulties each faces, what they need from each other to deliver consistent service and openly reviewing service problems together in a no blame atmosphere. Knowledge sharing would probably involve the development of practical processes for speeding up the exchange of good practice – for example, a 'What works in service' web site or an annual good practice fair. Communication professionals can support top management by helping them identify opportunities to demonstrate service values in action, or to listen to customers and employees discussing service quality issues.

The strategic process is not confined to the business level, however. While the business imposes a broad strategic direction, the implementation demands that each unit and each function develop its own, complementary, strategy. Iteration between these strategies, during their development, shapes the business plan.

The four pillars of communication therefore apply equally to each of these substrategies. If, for example, HR's strategy emphasizes the retention of staff, clarity of purpose demands that all managers understand the issue and what they have to do to keep their people. Trust development might involve giving managers the tools to have more open dialogue with individual employees about their concerns, their career prospects and other relevant issues. Knowledge sharing could include helping HR communicate information on salary competitiveness, and top management could be encouraged to demonstrate support for family-friendly policies and/or diversity programmes.

Similarly, the financial strategy could be better implemented with support from the communication function to raise people's general level of financial literacy, to give teams feedback about the cost of waste from their operations, and so on.

Pairing off the pillars

Although there is some small overlap between the four pillars, in general they describe four clearly defined activity areas. The question 'What happens when one or more pillars is absent?' was only marginally addressed in our study, but has since been an issue for exploration. The short cases below shed some light on the question, from an anecdotal point of view. For a more analytical view, however, we have found it useful to examine the pillars as a series of twinned interactions.

Clarity of purpose, when combined with top management communication behaviour, gives rise to Table 1.1.

Table 1.1 Top management communication behaviour

Sensitive *Top management* *behaviour*	CARING BUT INCOMPETENT	*CARING AND* *COMPETENT*
Driven *Top management* *behaviour*	INCOMPETENT AND UNCARING	*COMPETENT* *BUT UNCARING*
	Low *Clarity of purpose*	*High* *Clarity of purpose*

By caring, we mean that the business leaders are passionate about the business and are genuinely concerned for the welfare of the people in it. By competent, we mean that they are perceived to have a clear sense of direction and purpose, along with the ability to carry it out (i.e. they know what they are doing). Feeding back employee perceptions to top management using the matrix in Table 1.1 is a very powerful means of getting the message across, especially if the score is not in the caring and competent box!

In organizations with high levels of knowledge sharing and strong clarity of purpose, there should be very positive attitudes and capabilities for change (Table 1.2). When either pillar is weak, there is a high probability of either duplicated effort or a great deal of effort being expended on the wrong things. When both are weak, the ability to make things happen economically and coherently is greatly reduced.

Table 1.2 Clarity of purpose versus knowledge sharing

High *Knowledge sharing*	'WASTED EFFORT'	RAPID AND FOCUSED CHANGE – 'ON THE BALL'
Low *Knowledge sharing*	CHANGE DRIFT – 'ALL AT SEA'	'ILL JUDGED'
	Low *Clarity of purpose*	*High* *Clarity of purpose*

Where the organization has high levels of trust, particularly between teams and between employees and top management, combined with a clear sense of direction, there is a sense of collective energy. With trust but poor clarity of purpose, a cosy kind of club emerges, rather like that, which might be found in an old-fashioned legal practice, where everyone does their own thing. Where trust is low, but the clarity of purpose is high, people co-operate as long as it suits them. Although they are driving ahead to the same broad agenda, they also have their own private agendas in the background. Backbiting and political manoeuvring are common indicators of this kind of culture, but they are kept largely in check by the self-interest of achieving the common goals. (For example, the CEO of a health-care company ruled by fear, but kept his team united and focused with the promise of personal financial independence when the company was floated.)

Where there is neither trust nor clarity of purpose, the organization is at war with itself. Internal strife derails well-intentioned strategies and working together in harmony happens by exception rather than as the norm. This results in difficulties ranging from open warfare to complex political intrigue which detracts from (when it is not actively sabotaging) the task in hand.

Summary: so where does all this take us?

Making a major shift in the role of the communication function is not easy. Not least because doing so requires the co-operation of other people in the organization, who may have a fixed and traditional view of how communication supports the business. The good news is that the majority of experienced internal communication professionals respond to the research results by saying that this confirms what they have long suspected but not previously been able to articulate in a manner convincing to top management.

In this chapter, we have provided a basic background to the four pillars and some insights into how they influence the organization. From Chapter 4 onwards, we explore in greater detail a number of strategically important situations, where the internal communication function has a contribution to make. In each of those situations, building the communication response around the four pillars is an essential starting point in ensuring that the communication activity delivers the business results required.

References

Goldsmith, W. and Clutterbuck, D. (1984). *The Winning Streak*. Weidenfeld and Nicolson.

Goldsmith, W. and Clutterbuck, D. (1998). *The Winning Streak Mark II*. Weidenfeld and Nicolson.

Likert, R. (1961). *New Patterns of Management*. McGraw-Hill.

Loveman, G., Heskett, J. L., Jones, T. O., Schlesinger, L. A. and Sasser, W. E. (1994). Putting the service-profit chain to work. *Harvard Business Review*, March.

Peters, T. J. and Waterman, R. H. (1982). *In Search of Excellence*. Harper and Row.

Tichy, N. M. and Sherman, S. (1993). *Control your Destiny or Someone Else Will*. Doubleday.

Some core tools and concepts in employee communication

In this chapter, we examine some of the core concepts of effective communication management – in particular receptivity, interactive measurement, reputation management and sustaining dialogue. One thing these all have in common is that they do not often figure prominently (or in many cases at all) in the business's communication plan. Yet without a deep understanding of these concepts and how they apply to the individual organization, it is impossible for the communication professional to leverage the power of effective communication in support of the business' priorities.

Receptivity: turning on and tuning in

> *Receptivity is the process, in which people attend to, process and filter what they hear.*

Receptivity varies according to:

- the receiver's interest in the topic. (Is it relevant to me? Does it trigger any specific connections for me?) For example, visiting a new country, or establishing a relationship with someone from there, often provides a mental link that alerts the brain to references to that place. The more points of association you have with the place, the more likely you are to respond with attention, even if you then dismiss the information as irrelevant.

- the perceived urgency of the message, in the perception of the receiver. In direct speech, we convey urgency through the tone, speed and volume of communication. Newspapers deal with the same problem and so on through banner headlines and e-mails may attach a red exclamation mark. However, misuse of the urgent signal (again, as perceived by the receiver) makes it less effective.
- the receiver's conscious or unconscious emotions towards the topic. (Do I feel pleasure, discomfort or neutral thinking about this?) We are generally much more likely to pay attention to topics we find pleasurable than those we find painful. However, when the communication concerns something, about which we have a high level of fear, then we will tend to 'switch on' as our survival mechanisms take over.
- the receiver's attitude towards the transmitter. (Do they view the source as credible and well intentioned?)
- the timing of the communication. It is a lot easier to concentrate at some times than at others. In general, people are less likely to absorb information when their attention is focused on a close deadline or when they are working at full stretch.
- the receiver's general emotional state. (Are they relaxed, or under stress?)
- the meaning – both intellectual and emotional – that the receiver attaches to key words and phrases. For example, the word 'committee' may be very neutral to the sender, but may conjure up a picture of bureaucracy, time-wasting and boredom to the receiver, based on their previous experience and preconceptions. When communication crosses cultural divides, then this problem can be greatly exacerbated.
- people's individual preference, for *how* they receive information. (For example, do they respond best to text, to visual representations, or a mixture of both?)

Receptivity to a specific message is therefore far from uniform. The same message can be filtered in very different ways by different groups of people. Therefore, it is important to segment the various internal audiences according to their likely receptivity *to specific messages* prior to their transmission.

Assuming that everyone targeted with the message has received it and absorbed it is like assuming that everyone who has a television set will watch the same programme. This is not

Table 2.1 A sample receptivity map

Audience segment	Message content					
	Company goals and ambitions	Quality processes	Teamwork	Current work priorities	Environmental issues	Cost-cutting
Accounts	Low	Low	Moderate	Moderate	Low	High
IT	Low	Moderate	High	High	Low	Low
Marketing	High	Low	Low	High	Moderate	Low
Production	Low	High	High	High	Moderate	Moderate
Shop floor	etc.	etc.	etc.	etc.	etc.	etc.
Graduates						
Supervisors						

even remotely true. Receptivity management requires considerable upfront work to map out people's receptivity to different types of message (Table 2.1). Because of the effort involved it is unlikely there will be sufficient resource to develop individual receptivity maps (except for top management, where it may be essential, in terms of influencing them!), but it is usually possible to do so for departments (e.g. finance or sales and marketing), for particular demographic groups (e.g. women, ethnic minorities, graduates, middle managers, employees in different locations), or for people who have come from different organizations after a merger.

The simplest and cheapest way to develop receptivity maps is to carry out a mixture of focus groups and telephone interviews with a reasonable sample of each audience. Some companies achieve this with minimum effort by initiating brief discussions during training events or at other times when people gather away from the workplace. However it is done, the key is that this should be a pre-emptive activity – when a crisis occurs, there usually will not be the time for this kind of analysis.

Interactive measurement – how long *is* a piece of string?

Although most companies pay lip-service to the need to measure employee attitudes, the methods used are still for the most part relatively crude. Putting the standard employee attitude survey on line may improve its efficiency, but it is still just an attitude survey. Moreover, an annual or two-yearly survey has very limited value in terms of practical action. Like an annual report, it is a snapshot in time and very quickly out of date.

One of the most common confusions we encounter is between the employee attitude survey and the communication audit. The employee attitude survey aims to assess how people in the organization think and feel about it as an employer and as a place to work. A communication audit aims to establish how efficiently the various media and communication processes are working. Many organizations try to shoehorn these into a single survey. As a result, respondents may be confused about the purpose of the survey and the document can become sufficiently long to discourage people from completing it.

A third, related type of survey now appearing in some organizations is the values survey. This explores:

- the degree, to which employees endorse and are prepared to commit to the business or brand values
- how well they understand the values
- how they perceive their own and other people's behaviour, in terms of living the values
- the barriers they perceive in living the values.

A good practice approach to communication measurement:

- provides a *continuing* picture of the effectiveness of communication
- focuses on relatively few issues, consistently
- allows, in addition, for frequent micro-surveys on an ad hoc basis.

Reputation management – you are who you seem to be

Most of the research and practical experience around reputation management focuses on external reputation – how the company is seen by investors and other key stakeholders. However, reputation management is a core competence in relation to the internal stakeholders as well. There seem to be at least three levels here.

At the top of the organization, the reputation of the leaders has an enormous impact on motivation, clarity of purpose and the behaviour of other people. According to research by Richard Ruch (1979) for the Ford Motor Company, two factors consistently stand out in this context: employee perceptions of whether top management knows what it is doing, and of how much they *care*.

At the departmental level, reputation is a major factor in what resources a function receives (both financial and talent), whether it is part of the 'inner cabinet' of decision-making and its capacity to influence the thinking of top management. A study by **item** of the reputation of Human Resources found major differences in perception of the function by line manager internal customers. In some cases, HR was seen as a key partner in achieving the manager's objectives; in others, as a deadweight, or worse, as a significant barrier to achievement. Several factors emerged as important in the management of reputation with internal customers:

- personal characteristics and communication skills of the function's director or equivalent
- communications approach of the function
- demonstrated performance of the function in critical areas recognized by line managers as important
- the ability of the function to overcome both functional and geographical separation
- the ability of the function to add value to line managers by keeping them informed.

At the individual level, personal reputation has a defining influence on the career fortunes of ambitious people, whether they are young graduates or seasoned managers. Among the critical factors here are:

- being associated with successful, high-profile projects
- being perceived as competent in the core work you do
- the ability to be noticed (having a presence)
- being well networked
- being proactive in volunteering for interesting challenges and, somewhat paradoxically,
- knowing when to refuse assignments.

Dialogue or dire-log?

The typical internal communication function spends in excess of 90 per cent of its time and money on primarily one-way communication activities from the centre outwards – employee newspapers, e-zines, web sites, videos and so on. Most of the remainder is spent on two-way media, such as team briefings, and on one-way processes into the centre, such as employee opinion surveys. Very little, if any, is spent on promoting genuine dialogue.

> ## Debate, discussion and dialogue
>
> *Often used interchangeably, these three terms have very different meanings.*
>
> *Debate = having a fixed point of view and trying to convince others that it is right. Debate usually results in* entrenching existing views *and* resistance to change.
>
> Discussion = having an outcome you wish to achieve, but being willing to listen and accept the other person's view. Discussion typically leads to modest changes in perception, *and to* compromise.
>
> *Dialogue = approaching an issue with as open a mind as possible, with a view to understanding other people's perspectives and perhaps creating a new perspective. Dialogue typically leads to* commitment *and* willingness to change.

Why does that matter? Because all four of the key pillars of communication are seriously weakened in the absence of dialogue. Let us take each in turn.

Clarity of purpose

The capacity of people to misunderstand and to assign untrue motives to others is vast. The filters of personal experience, prejudice and culture distort even simple messages, unless there is an opportunity to question, probe and *explore meaning together.*

The lower the receptivity to the message, the greater the need for dialogue, to build understanding around the true intentions and vision. A half-hour of genuinely open dialogue between a leader and a small group of followers is worth a stack of videos, for example.

Trusting interfaces

Why do effective politicians spend so much time meeting people face to face? Because they know that they can build rapport with them far more easily than using a remote medium such as television. Creating and sustaining dialogue between groups of people in an organization is essential for social cohesion and teamwork. Whenever two functions impact upon each other's work, or compete for resources, mutual suspicion and resentment will occur – unless there is a process to encourage frequent dialogue.

Take the apparently straightforward statement 'I have no intention of closing any of our European factories'. Questions that will shape people's reactions, yet in most companies would never be asked openly, might include:

- 'You might not intend it, but what are your bosses in the USA planning?'
- 'They may not be closed, but will they be gradually run down?'
- 'Do you mean for the next few months, the next few years, for ever . . . ?'

Information exchange

Few organizations or the people within them have any shortage of information. What they lack, for the most part, is access to the right information, in the right form, at the right time. Promoting dialogue:

- makes people aware of the information needs of others around the organization
- makes people aware of who holds or is a gateway to particular types of information
- shares understanding about what information is important and what is not
- relates information availability more closely to current priorities for the organization.

In a study of the interfaces between a finance function and its internal customers, a significant factor in the poor relationships was that the latter resented the time they had to spend providing data, for which they could see little use or benefit in their own work. 'I could be using this time selling,' said one manager. Creating dialogue between them allowed the finance function to explain how vital the information was, what problems the internal customers would experience if the information was not gathered and how some of the problems they were already having were linked to late or inaccurate data. Understanding the customers' concerns, however, resulted in changes to the data collecting process and to the way it was fed back, making it of more immediate use and relevance to the running of the other departments.

Top management communication behaviour

The more aloof top management is perceived to be, the lower its credibility and reputation. Simply walking the floor is not enough. What makes the difference is the ability to engage people in meaningful discussion and demonstrate a genuine willingness to listen and reflect upon what the leader has heard. Great leaders in today's businesses are not people who will talk to you, but people who will talk *with you*.

Genuine dialogue:

- starts from a premise that there is value in understanding other people's perspectives
- aims to explore meaning together
- occurs when all parties are open to learning from each other
- takes place over time
- requires an atmosphere of quiet reflection.

You will see from this definition that the frenetic activity of a change event 'circus' is not genuine dialogue. Yes, people have the opportunity to 'hear it from the horse's mouth' and to discuss the implications of changes. But, as we shall see in Chapter 6 on change communication, it takes time and reflection for under-standing and behaviour change to take root at anything more than a superficial level. More often than not, companies exhaust their change communication budget on a slick, highly impressive event, with dry ice and exhilarating speeches. Then they are disappointed when the fervour of the day dissipates amid the reality of the working place.

Before running such an event, the internal communication professional – and the top team, who assign the budget – should consider:

- how much time is allowed for thinking? (Most events are organized to keep people active – for which read entertained – the entire time. This leaves no time for ideas to sink in and be subjected to internal critical review.)
- how will we sustain enthusiasm? (Instead of reaching a peak of hype on the day, it may be better to build a higher level of understanding on the day and use subsequent activities in the workplace gradually to ramp up the levels of commitment and excitement.)

Dialogue does not have to be face to face. The value of e-dialogue is becoming clearer as more top management teams engage and involve people throughout the business in thinking about business issues. A practical process might involve a monthly topic, with the issues presented in brief by the leader, who owns them, and with access to further data on a web site. The responses – comments, ideas, criticisms and more information, contributed by the employees (and, in some cases, trusted outsiders) – are collated and summarized weekly in a form that stimulates further dialogue. At the end of the month, the leader thanks all the discussants, draws some conclusions, shares what they have learned and invites people to take part in the next dialogue, to be championed by another of the top team.

Team briefing – I have been told to tell you . . .

Similarly, the team briefing approach adopted over the past forty years or so is far from ideal in the modern team environment, and especially with those types of team where physical interaction between members is infrequent and often fleeting. Sometimes called cascade briefing, it is based on a core, regular set of messages distributed from top management and added to by other layers as it passes down the chain. The team briefing system allows for information to be adapted to the needs of groups or departments, and may convey information more effectively than print media because of the element of personal contact and employee involvement.

However, many organizations' team briefings suffer from inconsistency – although the information distributed may be the same, the manner in which it is put across depends on the enthusiasm and communication skills of the team leader. In practice, most organizations struggle to get all managers to hold team briefings. If they impose sanctions upon managers who fail to brief, the process becomes mechanical and ineffective.

In theory, team briefing has a feedback loop, allowing for managers to gather employees' thoughts and opinions and pass them back through the levels to senior management. However, even where it works, this feedback is largely confined to questions about the issues raised in the briefing, rather than issues of concern to the briefees. Traditional team briefings' shortcomings include:

- focusing on what top management wants to tell, rather than on what people in the organization want to know
- timing based on top management's agenda, not that of the team
- a tendency towards the mechanical, with team leaders simply passing on information; as a result, little ownership of the information
- the very term 'briefing' indicates that this is meant to be a short, focused session, so there is neither time for nor expectation of a substantial discussion of the issues raised.

Various attempts have been made to make the information flow more two-way, focusing on discussion rather than on instruction. These typically encourage teams to spend more time talking about issues, but:

- the agenda still belongs primarily to top management
- informing top management about what people at other levels think does not necessarily lead to changes in policy; teams can quickly become disillusioned when they see that their opinion does not greatly matter in the larger scheme of things
- there is little incentive or process to deal with anything but surface issues, especially with regard to hidden conflict within the team
- the communication process remains heavily dependent on the competence and interest of the team leader.

In the context of the twenty-first-century workplace, both these approaches are struggling to make an impact. A number of evolutions in the working environment contribute to this.

Knowledge workers are becoming much more concerned about and motivated by having greater control of what they do and how they do it. The language of empowerment has been superseded by the more personalized rhetoric of influence and control.

Managers' attention is increasingly focused upwards rather than downwards. In leaner hierarchies, time to lead the team is constantly squeezed by the need to contribute to larger programmes of change. As a result, effective managers concentrate on *creating the climate where communication can happen*, rather than see themselves as the conduit between the team and the rest of the organization – less still between members of the team.

This change of style, combined with greater access to information of all kinds as a result of IT, places responsibility for communication increasingly on the receiver, not the sender. In the knowledge world, *everyone* is responsible for communicating.

As businesses become increasingly complex in structure, with roles and responsibilities changing rapidly, the opportunities for misunderstanding and for conflict of objectives increase. Add to this the exponential rise in working in cross-level, cross-division, cross-function, cross-culture, cross-time zone teams and communication becomes even more difficult to manage through any form of command and control. Just as the team leader now has to influence rather than control communication, so the leadership of the organization has to think in terms of harnessing and encouraging the informal communication systems rather than pushing messages through the formal systems.

As teams become scattered, often operating globally, the opportunity to bring people together in one place at one time occurs less frequently. Reliance on traditional methods of briefing is not enough. The emphasis of communication can become more and more transactional, rather than relationship building. Worse still, electronic communication is often substituting for face-to-face communication, with people a few yards away preferring to e-mail rather than talk to each other. McKinsey's have estimated that fewer than 5 per cent of teams actually perform more effectively than the individuals would have done on their own.

As the boundaries of organizations become more and more transparent, defining who should be within the communication umbrella becomes harder. Which subcontractors should be included, even though they are on someone else's payroll? What about staff of joint ventures with competitors? Where employees have to work very closely with customers' teams, should those teams also be in the loop?

With organizations relying increasingly on shared values to stimulate loyalty, commitment and sense of direction among employees, transactional information – the essence of team briefing – becomes less and less important. Electronic media are, arguably, more efficient, more timely and more accurate for transferring information, and for collecting direct feedback of employee's views. The development of shared values depends not on briefing or discussion, but on genuine and continued *dialogue*.

Why team briefing needs to give way to team dialogue

The concept of *team dialogue* is a logical evolution of team communication and a pragmatic response to changes in the organizational and team environment. It represents a major shift of emphasis that allows both for the internalization of messages and ideas, and for the development of a deeper level of shared understanding. It also encourages constructive challenge and the taking of initiative, with or without the active involvement of the team leader.

Among the benefits of the approach are that it:

- supports and reinforces team learning (and hence, ultimately the development of a learning organization)
- contributes to three of the four key activities that link communication activity to business success (clarity of purpose, effective interfaces, effective information sharing and leadership behaviour; IABC, 2001) – all four, if the top team is prepared to engage in and demonstrate team dialogue for itself

- directly reinforces the translation of values into action, providing well-thought-through feedback on conflict between the stated values and what the organization and its people actually do
- promotes commitment from both the individual and the team
- actively encourages the team to bring to the surface those issues (internal or external) which are too uncomfortable to discuss under normal circumstances – for example, questioning the fundamentals of a project approach, or behaviour of the team leader.

The rules of team dialogue are simple:

- Meetings occur when the team has something to discuss. This may be some information from above, or to share some learning gained by individual members, or to consider a practical issue of work management.
- The team leader may or may not facilitate the discussion; the team itself decides who should take the facilitator role.
- The goal of the meeting is to create first shared understanding, then shared meaning.
- Everyone has something to contribute, because everyone has to take ownership of the outcomes.
- Everyone's views and values must be respected, especially when they are significantly different from your own.
- There are no individual winners, no individual losers, no compromises. The team wins when it acquires a deeper understanding of issues and a consensus about how to tackle them.

The team dialogue process – suspending beliefs

The skills of team dialogue need to be learned. For the team leader, accustomed to giving instruction, it can be difficult to take a back seat. He or she may also find it uncomfortable to receive direct or indirect criticism from the team. However, there are considerable payoffs, in being able to delegate far more than he or she might normally expect.

For the team member, the core skills of team dialogue include:

- starting with an open mind – an intention to learn first, even if you already have some strong views
- focusing on building your own understanding – e.g. how does a colleague's view differ from your own? What beliefs or

values are they applying? What logic lies behind the difference? How does their experience differ from your own?

- being open about your perspectives and how they are derived
- seeing an issue both in the micro (what it means to me/us) and the macro (what it means to the organization/our customers)
- showing appreciation for each other's openness and trust
- being prepared to become the leader/facilitator, when your ideas have the floor, and to relinquish gracefully the role to someone else.

Some good practice ideas in managing team dialogue include:

- inviting people from other teams to join the meeting as observers or participants, to introduce a wider perspective
- proactively seeking input from senior management, to inform the dialogue and ensure it is linked to the political reality of the organization
- starting with relatively non-contentious issues to build people's confidence in the process and gradually progressing to more difficult topics
- always beginning by relating topics to the team and/or business objectives; and to the shared values.

Getting to dialogue

Given that most managers have not yet mastered traditional team briefing, it may seem optimistic to expect them to embrace team dialogue. Yet, in many ways, team dialogue is an easier sell at the work-face. It meets the need of knowledge workers to exert more control over their working environment; it frees the team leader to concentrate on other priorities; and it addresses issues in the team's time frame. However, team dialogue takes longer than briefing and requires quality time – reflective space – which can be hard to find in a task-driven organization.

The future of team dialogue therefore depends on the perspective an organization takes on investing in its future. It seems that teams – of all varieties – will remain the backbone of organizations for the coming decades. To maintain competitive advantage, therefore, companies will need to make radical improvements in team performance. While new technology still has some potential to influence performance improvement, it can realistically only do so by raising the quantity and quality of team communication.

Internal communication as an enabler

This is a theme we have already referred to in Chapter 1 and will return to again. It is not possible to hold a conversation for someone, or to empower him or her or to change their inner beliefs. The best we can do is to give them the necessary tools, environment and encouragement. The tools are primarily the communication competencies, enhanced through appropriate training and personal feedback, and access to relevant media. The environment consists of a mixture of organizational climate, structure, geographical dispersion and culture. Encouragement

Table 2.2 Checklist used for benchmarking

	SCORE Very true ——————— Not true				
1 We spend a great deal of effort in helping people talk to each other	5	4	3	2	1
2 Our employee newspaper/e-zine is designed to put people in contact with each other	5	4	3	2	1
3 We play an active role in helping top management engage employees in discussion on topical issues	5	4	3	2	1
4 Most of the IC staff act as internal consultants rather than deliverers	5	4	3	2	1
5 We play an active role in communication training	5	4	3	2	1
6 We maintain a register of formal and informal interest groups	5	4	3	2	1
7 Our budget places a very low emphasis on one-way media	5	4	3	2	1
8 Line managers see us as there to advise them on how to handle communications issues, not to communicate for them	5	4	3	2	1
9 We spend a great deal of effort listening to employees	5	4	3	2	1
10 We help managers get feedback about their performance as communicators	5	4	3	2	1

comes from the recognition and praise awarded by top management for good communication behaviours; and from the benefits that people observe, when they do communicate well.

A short checklist to benchmark your function on its role as an enabler is given in Table 2.2.

If you score more than thirty, your function is well on the way to performing an enabling role. Between eighteen and thirty, you need to build some clarity and commitment about the enabling role, but you have at least the basis for achieving it. If you score seventeen or under, you are most likely trapped in a role that assumes communication is something you do to people, rather than something you help them do for themselves.

Summary

If internal communication is to be truly business focused, it has to move rapidly from being input focused to being output focused. It must work from the realities and needs of the internal audience, seeking to understand their receptivity and supporting the creation of communities of dialogue that cut across departmental, hierarchical and geographical boundaries. It must also shift the emphasis of its funding towards dialogue and away from monologue.

References

International Association of Business Communicators (IABC) (2001). *Investigating the Link between Communication Competence and Business Success*. IABC.

Ruch, R. (1979). *International Management*, December, 33–37.

CHAPTER 3

The internal community of communication

This chapter examines the business case for internal communication in more detail and looks at how communication actually happens in organizations. The proportion of communication that is under the control of the internal communication function is very small – typically only a few per cent. So how can a small department affect the quality of communication more widely? Every other function and activity in the business needs to communicate, but how does it learn to do so more effectively, and how can the IC function help?

We refer to the internal community of communication because it is generally a helpful metaphor. Communities consist of groups of people, who may have many differences, yet have enough purpose in common to accept each other, to co-operate with each other, to share with each other and to learn from each other. A community exists in a state of relative harmony, compared with the outside world, with each individual having both a sense of how they fit in and a feeling of belonging. So this chapter also seeks to provide insights into how the communication function can help build both the quality and the quantity of meaningful exchange throughout the internal community.

Functions versus activities

Although most businesses have organizational charts that emphasize functional silos, it would be impossible for them to survive if they really behaved that way. It would simply take too long for messages to work through the hierarchy and the capacity for error would be enormous. In all but a handful of companies, many important aspects of the business – from property management to clarifying the corporate strategy – fall across or between silos.

Matrix management structures attempt to overcome the problem by giving people dual or multiple reporting lines. While this typically improves communication generally, it also tends to create confusion about priorities and who has primary responsibility for key tasks.

In non-matrix organizations, what actually happens is that the whole process relies upon people subverting the system, and in general, it works surprisingly well. People find opportunities and ways to talk with those in other functions, who can be helpful to them. People learn to reciprocate, by being helpful, because staying aloof from this process of social exchange would make it more difficult for them to get the information and exert the influence they need to do their jobs.

The internal communication function cannot control, nor even know about most of this activity. But it can encourage and provide the framework, under which it can flourish. It does so in two ways: by assisting *key influencing communities* to communicate more effectively and by supporting a *positive communication climate*. Key influencing communities may be clearly structured and formal – for example, functions such as HR or IT – or diffuse and relatively informal – such as the managers and others involved in the evolution of strategy. To shorten these, we can describe the two types as functions and activities. Functions tend to have history, an enduring set of responsibilities and permanent staff. Activities involve people from across the business, often in addition to their functional responsibilities.

We shall consider the issues surrounding positive communication climate later in the chapter, but for now let us concentrate on key influencing communities. A helpful way of looking at this complex set of interactions is seen in Table 3.1.

The four activities identified here can be argued to be generic and core to all businesses. While individual businesses may wish to add others, we have met few, if any, that could afford to ignore any of these and still prosper.

Targeted communication activity is essential in each of the boxes in Table 3.1. There is not space here to explore in depth how

Table 3.1 Functions versus activities matrix

| | Function | | | | | |
Activity	Finance	Human resources	Sales/ marketing	Operations	Research	Other
Setting strategic intent						
Business planning						
Change management						
Handling the psychological contract						

this is achieved, and in any case the solution must be chosen with a view to the organization's own requirements. This matrix simply provides a focus for the communicator's thinking and for discussion with top management. However, it is not enough simply to find activities to fill all the boxes. At the same time, an integrated vision and communication plan must tie all of this diverse activity together.

The essence of internal communication management is therefore the judicious combination of autonomy, to allow each function and/or activity to communicate its own messages in its own way, and integration, to ensure that people within and outside the organization understand how each element fits into the big picture. The potential for getting the balance wrong is huge. For example, centralized control has created frustration for one finance company whose UK-based communicators are forced to follow the format determined by the USA-based centralized function, even when that includes information which is clearly irrelevant to the British team.

On the other hand, another major financial services company has recently successfully combined its communication functions across the organization, having realized that vast amounts of effort were being duplicated by the teams working independently to communicate the same initiatives to their own divisions. Communication management can make a major difference to the performance of the four key activities and of the functions when they operate independently of each other. Where they meet, the potential to exert positive influence is multiplied. Let us start by looking at the relationship between internal communication and each of the activities.

How employee communication can help clarify strategic intent

Strategic intent describes the basket of activities, which enable the leadership of an organization to build a deep and clear consensus about what they want the business to achieve, the broad strategy for getting there, and the shared beliefs that underpin the choices they will make and the behaviours they will demonstrate en route. This process occurs at a corporate level, where the executives contribute from the dual perspective of their area of functional responsibility and the helicopter view of the bigger picture. It also occurs at functional level, where, say, the HR team develops its own sense of strategic intent, which is at the same time both constrained by the corporate view and independent of it. (For example, HR professionals will often experience a dual loyalty, to the organization and to the employees, that may provide a moderating influence on the 'hard' business case.)

A strong sense of strategic intent is invaluable in generating clarity of purpose. It provides at least partial immunization against day-to-day deviations from or shifts in strategy or policy. It also radiates invisibly, so that people throughout the organization absorb the reasoning and the patterns of assumption behind the strategy unconsciously. The ground is therefore well prepared when the concepts and ambitions are articulated consciously.

In communication management terms, the development of strategic intent requires the communication function to work with the top team to understand the business drivers, vision and values, and how the communication function can best support the business, both at the corporate and at the operational level.

At the corporate level, the communication manager can help the top team to:

- explore meaning at the top. (Do people have the same mental models? Do they have the same understanding of the priorities?)
- make the link between vision with values
- define the benefits of a strategy for all the stakeholders.

At the operational level, the communication function requires processes to:

- communicate the strategy, vision and values and the links between them
- demonstrate the benefits of the strategy to the stakeholders
- manage the metaphor: create differentiation in terms that excite people and help them see how they can play a part in achieving the strategic goals
- generate and discuss feedback on how the strategy is actually being carried out (and, in particular, to distinguish between the letter and the spirit of compliance).

With few exceptions, these processes will only occur where there is regular, insightful and challenging dialogue between the internal communication professionals and the whole of the top team.

How employee communication interfaces with change management

Managing change is one of the most important and most challenging roles for communicators. During change, employees are hungry for information about what will alter and how it will affect them, yet the full implications of change are rarely clear before the event, and where they are clear there are frequently barriers to communicating them, whether it is the regulatory issues surrounding a merger or the need to time announcements appropriately. The implications of change for the communicator are dealt with in much greater detail in Chapter 6, 'Communicating during radical change'. In particular, we explore the process of individual change which must underpin any shift in organizational culture, and the role the communicator can play in facilitating individual change.

How employee communication interfaces with business planning

A major European food manufacturer informed employees on one of its production lines that, while they were away on a two-week vacation, their processing line was to be ripped out and replaced with the latest equipment, and that they should be prepared to spend time retraining on their return. No jobs were to be lost, but the employees still felt concerned that they only learned of this change a few days before their vacation was due to begin. They made fond farewells to the old machinery and were greeted on their return with a new, quieter and apparently more efficient line, dominated by a giant processor.

Within three days, the top half of the new processor was in pieces. Not because of any mechanical fault, but because food hygiene regulations demanded that certain mechanical parts be cleaned frequently. Unfortunately, the positioning of the machinery meant that it was too close to the wall, so the operators were unable safely to gain the internal access they needed. Shutting down and moving the equipment cost three days' production – equivalent to about half the annual salary of the operating team.

The company learnt its lesson. Now, whenever there is a change in equipment, it consults the operators fully, recognizing that they are more likely to spot the practical problems than engineers who do not have to work the equipment day in and day out.

Although this mechanical problem was hardly an issue of great strategic importance, it illustrates the problem that all organizations have in making business plans that work. No matter how good or bad the overall planning assumptions are, the devil is in the detail. And the detail typically belongs to the people who are at the end of the decision-making chain. Turning that chain into a loop – a constant dialogue about intention and reality – is a communication task, which can be facilitated by developing and maintaining channels between the planners and the doers. Even simple devices, such as a 'Plans and targets' web site, can make a big difference. Professional communicators can also play a mediation role in bringing planners and doers together when things go wrong, helping both sides develop better processes that will reduce the danger of similar problems in the future.

Such help is even more relevant in the macho world of everlasting quarterly profit increases, where tough targets are set against a spoken or unspoken expectation of 'This is the goal we've set. Your job is to do what it takes to make it happen'. Short cuts, compromises and stress are inevitable effects of such an approach. Leaving aside how sustainable this is (and spectacular collapses are often examples of what happens when cultures take this behaviour to extremes), the tougher the targets, the greater the need for information, involvement and discussion.

How employee communication interfaces with the psychological contract

According to Gallup's ongoing research into employee motivation (Buckingham, 2001), 80 per cent of employees are not engaged at work. The reasons for this are many, but at the core lies a disconnection between the expectations the organization has of its people, and the expectations they have of the organization. These combined expectations are commonly referred to as the psychological contract.

Very rarely is the psychological contract a formal, clearly articulated set of expectations. On the contrary, it tends to be a mixture of emotional and intellectual expectations, which may or may not be mutually understood, and which derive in large part from the values important to each stakeholder group. A positive psychological contract tends to exist when:

- there is an alignment of values between the organization and the stakeholders concerned
- both parties feel valued by each other.

Reams have been written to explain the psychological contract as a concept, but the simplest and most effective way is to focus on the three different meanings of value depicted in the values triangle in the Introduction:

- Worth (The creation of value-added. For the organization, this is frequently focused on shareholder value-added. For the individual employee, it may involve a mixture of reward/compensation, training and opportunities to gain experience, which improve their value in the job market. For the customer, worth is often related to value for money.)
- Respect (As in 'I value your contribution/your custom' or 'I feel proud to say I work for this company'.)
- Belief (What people believe to be important – the values that underlie decisions and behaviours. For example, at Body Shop or Patagonia, employees, managers and customers share common beliefs about the importance of environmental considerations.)

Employee retention and motivation are both closely related to:

- how fair and even-handed the psychological contract is perceived to be
- how well the psychological contract terms are lived up to, in the perception of each party.

This in turn will impact other shareholders and may affect customer goodwill or stakeholder loyalty. The damage that can be done by breaking the usually unwritten contract is often badly underestimated by top management.

Even small changes can have an enormous impact on the level of real and perceived trust between managers and employees. For example, in one telemarketing company senior management began to enforce the ruling that staff should not use company telephones and Internet connections for personal reasons – previously there had been an unspoken agreement with line managers that employees were permitted an 'acceptable level' of personal calls and Internet access. Employees felt that the strict enforcement of the rule demonstrated a lack of trust on the part of senior management, and motivation plummeted.

The communication function has an important role in both clarifying the psychological contract and providing feedback (in either direction) when it appears to be breaking down. Once again, the key lies in generating the kind of dialogue that allows people to share expectations and express their concerns when they feel the psychological contract is not being kept.

Linking the activities together

Effective communication management also provides the interface, by which all four of these cross-company activities integrate with each other (Figure 3.1). In theory, strategic intent should lead directly to business planning, which in turn should generate change projects. The impact of these on the psychological contract should be under constant review. In practice, what actually happens is that top management generates the strategic intent and leaves the bulk of business planning and change management to middle managers. No one takes responsibility for the psychological contract, because it does not appear on the organizational chart and is not measured anyway.

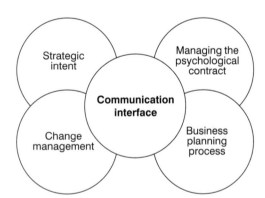

Figure 3.1 Communication as the key interface between organizational activities

The responsibility of the communication function is to raise awareness of these issues, provide measurement where practical and to seek to influence managers from all functions and activities to make communication a higher priority. This may be a difficult and thankless task, not least because it may not be asked for by those who stand to benefit from it. The active championship of the CEO is therefore a fundamental requirement in creating a community of communication.

Supporting other business functions

In approaching the communication needs of both activities and functions, keeping the four pillars of communication in mind will greatly assist in the delivery of measurable, successful outcomes. The starting point, however, for practical interventions is recognition of need by the partner function.

In general, functions within an organization allow communication to happen, rather than manage the process. Responsibility for communication is dispersed among the employees within the function and there is rarely an individual or team with the remit to monitor quality or impact. It is hardly surprising then, that the functions with the highest volume of communication activity – HR, finance and IT – are also those with the lowest reputation with colleagues for service quality (Azzolini and Lingle, 1993). Various research projects by **item** over the years (Clutterbuck and Dearlove, 1993) have demonstrated a link between a staff function's reputation and its ability to deliver the quality of services the business needs.

Convincing the leaders of a function of the need for more proactive communication management may require some initial investment in producing the kind of data that makes the case. Among practical processes for doing so are:

- comparison, through surveys, of the reputation of each function on a number of factors, such as service quality to internal customers, professionalism and business orientation
- gathering information on the cost of specific communication failures, in terms of money, lost opportunities and missed deadlines
- mining existing data sources, such as quality measures, labour retention statistics and employee opinion surveys (although the latter often tend not to ask the function specific questions).

Clarity of purpose

Clarity of purpose is as essential to a function as to the business as a whole. What is the function there for? How does it contribute to the performance of the business and to the performance of other functions? These two questions (which, of course, the IC function has to answer for itself as well) need to be answered in a way that is meaningful to both the internal customer and the employees, who work in the function. Creating a form of words that can be distributed as a statement of vision and values is the easy part. Persuading the internal audiences that there is substance behind the words is more difficult – especially if their experience of interaction with the function is very different from the aspirations in the vision.

Part of the answer is to establish very clearly what the function does *not* do. Take the HR function. As Figure 3.2 indicates, it has four major areas of service, which it can offer: strategic or tactical, support or delivery. The probability of doing all these superbly well is remote. Yet if it does one badly, this will colour its reputation as a whole. Hence the decision of increasing numbers of HR functions to raise their reputation by concentrating only on those activities they know they can do well and either outsourcing or returning to the line everything else. This change is in itself a communication challenge!

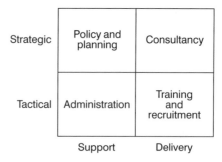

Figure 3.2 What business is the staff function in?

The same principle of clarity of focus applies to the internal communication function itself. The same box labels apply, with the exception of tactical delivery, in which one might put activities such as producing the employee publication, or running a biannual employee opinion survey. It will in most cases be very difficult for the function to deliver well consistently in all four areas and the area it performs least well in will most often drag down its reputation within the organization. Some clarity about where the organization most needs excellence can help shape the function, so that it puts its mental and financial resources where it can both perform well and have the maximum positive impact on the business.

Gaining the consent of top management and the understanding of internal customers to a focusing down of activity requires a great deal of patient discussion and explanation. A campaign approach helps in many cases and the manner, in which the function makes its case and manages the communication process will have a major effect on how receptive the internal customers are to the new situation and to the IC team. It can also help to take the decisions about what internal communication does and does not do down to a more detailed level.

The communication strategy matrix

The communication strategy matrix is a simple but effective planning process aimed at clarifying where employee communication activity can add value to the business, or to the individual function. It also provides a starting point for cost-benefit analysis of investment in communication activity.

The horizontal axis of the matrix consists of key *value-adding strategies or issues*. These may be:

- the critical business challenges for the coming 12–24 months
- the core elements of the business or functional strategy
- the business values

at either corporate, divisional or business function level.

Gaining clarity and total agreement on these elements is an essential first step, which addresses a critical question in terms of organizational communication competence: do the leaders know what they want to achieve and what priorities they wish to apply?

The vertical axis relates to the *communication purpose*. Does the organization or function wish to

- inform people (raise awareness)
- motivate them in the short term (i.e. a boost in enthusiasm)
- develop real understanding of the issues (so people target their enthusiasm where it will have most effect on building value)
- change behaviours/build long-term, sustained motivation.

Each box on the matrix represents an opportunity to use communication in pursuit of the horizontal goals. Some examples are shown in Table 3.2, again using the HR function as the internal customer.

Having identified communication-related issues, the team can now examine what degree of change it wishes to stimulate. In some acquisitions, for example, it may be enough simply to keep people informed – particularly, if nothing much will change for them. In general, *the minimum effective cost of communication* (the

Table 3.2 Functional strategy versus communication purpose

	Strategy			
Communication purpose	Customer retention	Employee retention among the top 500	Cost reduction	Integrating acquisitions rapidly
Inform	Make employees aware of customers at risk and the potential effect of their loss	Explain reward systems clearly	Communicate clear goals and the reasons for them	Share information about the organizations: structure, people and culture
Enthuse	Establish a clear link between their rewards and customer retention	Excite them about opportunities opening up	Introduce an element of fun	Help people see the benefits of the merger
Develop understanding	Involve employees in dialogue about how they can influence customer retention	Involve managers more deeply in thinking about strategic issues, to increase their sense of ownership Clarify the psychological contract	Involve them in dialogue about how they can influence cost savings	Establish networks for rapid sharing of knowledge, culture, etc.
Behaviour change/ long-term motivation	Provide role models, performance feedback, etc.	Support through mentoring and coaching	Develop a long-term attitude change	Provide feedback on behaviours

amount of money and time required to achieve the communication objective in the most cost-effective way) will change with the communication purpose.

Each of the communication-related issues can now be examined in terms of:

- the media/communication approaches available (from top management time to web sites or videos, for example)
- the cost-effectiveness of each of these approaches in achieving the communication purpose and the strategic objective.

It soon becomes clear where savings can be made by using the same mix of media to support several of the strategic priorities and where a more focused, discrete approach will be more appropriate.

The steps from informing to behaviour change represent a scale of both cost and impact. Least expensive, generally is simply keeping people informed, but this is unlikely to have much impact on the key business goals. Changing behaviour and motivating people long term is both more costly and more impactful on the business. However, in most cases, the cost-benefit equation improves as you move towards the more complex processes of behaviour change.

The communication strategy matrix opens up these discussions in a straightforward manner, allowing top managers to consider where and how much they want to invest in communication, and the implications of doing so. Gaining buy-in in this way (having been involved in the decision, it is hard for these managers to back out) both reinforces clarity of what is expected and obliges them to lend at least some support to the process. It also means that, because there is a clearer link between communication spend and business outcomes, managers are (a) more likely to invest appropriate resources and (b) less likely to cut resources for communication, for those outcomes, which they see as business priorities.

Top management communication behaviour

Your top team needs help! Those who are not good communicators need support and encouragement in developing their skills. Those who are good communicators need support in regaining where and how specific communication interventions on their part can make a real and significant difference to the fulfilment of a strategy – both in the broad picture and in their day-to-day activities.

Let us start with the example of the Human Resources director. Our studies of HR reputation also identified the key role played by the reputation of the leaders of the function. In those organizations, where line managers preferred to bypass HR, or perceived it to be generally unhelpful, the HR leaders were seen as aloof, insufficiently commercial or business aware, and lacking in proactivity. Human Resources managers, who were able to exert a positive influence on the organization and whose departments were seen by line managers as an important resource in helping them do their jobs, were characterized by:

- demonstrating that they understood the business issues through the eyes of the internal customer
- adapting their language to make things clear to internal customers (i.e. avoiding HR jargon)
- making the time to visit and talk with people in the operations, rather than expecting them to come to headquarters
- adapting the HR function's response times to the internal customer's perception of urgency, rather than their own
- making it easier for line managers to keep up to date on good practice in people management by doing the reading for them and presenting information and ideas in ways that suited the managers' ways of working
- making HR the guinea pigs for new ways of working (i.e. being seen to take their own medicine first)
- being highly respected by their own teams, in terms of professionalism and of concern for their staff.

Helping the functional leaders to consider these issues and develop their own reputation management plans is a relatively straightforward consultancy role. And, of course, the same basic factors will apply to the leaders of the internal communication function. Before offering to help other functions, it may be a wise move to assess perceptions within and outside the internal communication team on these or similar factors!

Trusting interfaces

MORI's research indicates that the more frequently people interact with a function, the more positive their attitude towards it. Familiarity, it seems, breeds respect.

Trusting interfaces between functions arise when:

- expectations are clear as to what each provides the other, and how
- each side understands the other's priorities and, motivations and fears

- there are frequent opportunities for discussion about service failures or potential problems
- people have time and opportunity to build relationships as well as conduct transactions.

Establishing and sustaining opportunities for dialogue between internal customers and providers should in theory be easy, but in practice it is often hard to achieve. People are simply too focused on achieving their own main tasks to build in the time to talk. Yet the continuous exchange of experience, perception and meaning is critical to the smooth operation of interfaces between functions.

The IC function can provide practical help in several ways, including:

- customer satisfaction surveys and focus groups
- helping internal customers and providers create opportunities for structured dialogue
- identifying gaps in the communication chain between functions at different levels in the hierarchy.

In particular, the internal communicators can help to soften the largely mechanical processes that characterize the information exchange approaches of many departments. For example, service level agreements have fallen into disrepute in many organizations because they have become a means to assign blame, rather than an opportunity to explore together ways to improve service quality. Enabling both sides to communicate more effectively reduces the tension and suspicion, so that they can concentrate on managing expectations and focus on practical improvements, in which both provider and customer have a role to play. A key element in such discussions is the open and frank exploration of what each party should reasonably be expected to put into the interaction in terms of money, time, mental effort (e.g. articulating and structuring problems to be tackled; generating ideas for resolving problems) and physical effort (e.g. who comes to whom).

Information sharing

For most functions, the primary problem they have with information sharing is not that they do not issue enough information, but that they flood people with too much, or that what they do provide is often contradictory. The internal communication professional should play an active role in helping other functions think through how they will limit the volume of communication, while improving the quality. A European retailer, for example, found that messages from headquarter's functions were taking up between two and three hours per day of store managers' time. One result of this was that managers were confused about what was most important for them to achieve; another was that they had insufficient time to pass information along to other employees. The solution was to persuade each function to follow some basic rules about

- identifying what was most important and urgent
- routing all communication through one daily channel and a much reduced set of less frequent media
- providing information that really needed to be circulated more widely in a form that made pass-along simpler.

It also instituted a measurement process that gave each department regular feedback about how its information flow was perceived by the managers. The results included a significant drop in 'junk' communication and an increase in the time the store managers spent communicating with their own staff.

Key questions for IC professionals

As we have indicated several times in this section, what applies to helping other functions communicate more effectively applies to the communication function itself. Basic questions every internal communication department should ask itself regularly include:

- What do our internal customers think of the service we provide?
- What do they think of how we provide those services?
- Can we demonstrate satisfactorily that we are investing resources in activities that support the business's strategic priorities?
- Are we resourced and structured to give other functions the support they need?

This last question raises an additional issue. In communication strategy workshops, we have often found that internal communication specialists deliberately hold back from promoting the function's capabilities within the organization. 'We couldn't cope with the flood of demand', is a surprisingly common statement. Such a tactical, short-term response loses the opportunity to build the professional reputation of the communication function. It also usually means that the communicators are avoiding the high-level debate about where and how they can best add value to the business. Open communication requires that these issues are aired in a way that allows all the communicating functions to contribute to the discussion on the kind of help they need. Failure to do so is, in our view, an abdication of the professional communicator's responsibilities.

Developing a positive communication climate

The communication climate, like the air around us, permeates every aspect of communication. Focusing solely on activities and functions is like going to keep-fit sessions without giving up smoking. To make a real and lasting difference to the quality of communication within an organization, you have to pay attention to the context in which it takes place. People's behaviours, expectations and commitment to the business and each other will be radically different in a positive communication climate than in a negative one.

Academics argue vehemently over the concept of climate – whether it is real and, if so, whether it is measurable. For the communication practitioner, however, it is not difficult to gain a sense of whether communication is, for example, open and natural or restrained and guarded.

The factors that contribute to the nature of a communication climate are many. Among the most important, however, are:

- Rivalry between leaders. When David Clutterbuck worked for McGraw-Hill in the UK, the publications company and the book company were on the second and first floors respectively. Contact between employees was tacitly discouraged by senior managers, who appeared to be concerned about information being 'leaked' back to headquarters in New York. Employees sat in the staff restaurant with their immediate working colleagues and all sorts of opportunities for collaboration were lost. It was the discovery that both divisions were investing effort into investigating the same new business venture that brought the founding of **item**, when the two editors-in-chief got together to plan their own, different venture. However, perhaps this demonstrates that the managers were right to attempt to isolate them!
- The instinctive reluctance of most people to seek social interaction with people outside their own community. Even where people have to interface with people in other departments or from other functions, communication tends to be on a transactional rather than a relationship-building basis. It takes a spark of common interest or a welcoming gesture by

one of the parties, to break through the protective membrane that surrounds most communities.

- The infrastructure may either support or hinder social exchange. Workers in US and European plants taken over by Japanese companies have typically found it difficult to develop relationships with their Japanese counterparts, even where there is ample opportunity to communicate by e-mail. Exchange visits, where employees from the different cultures were able to work alongside each other, have had a major positive effect in building relationships and hence in the quality and quantity of ideas exchanged.

Communication climate can vary considerably within the various divisions and sites of an organization, not least because these and other influencing factors will be different. However, the starting point for the communication professional must be the overall picture of the organization: is the communication climate positive or negative and where can improvements be made?

So how do you recognize and stimulate a positive communication climate? Table 3.3 provides some clues.

While most of these issues can be addressed in questionnaires, our experience is that greater insights come from discussing them in small focus groups, where it is possible to gather examples and to explore the implications of behaviours.

Having measured communication climate, however, what can the IC function do about it? One immediate lesson from fieldwork is that the power to change climate rests fairly equally with three parties:

- top management, who must make it clear that they expect open communication and who must become role models for it
- line managers, who must overcome their own fears to do the same
- the individual employee, who must be prepared to step into the unknown and build bridges to people and communities with whom they would not normally engage.

What the communication function cannot do is change people's behaviour for them. It can, however, constantly make the case for openness and inclusivity, educate people at all levels in the organization about the benefits of linking communities and creating new communities, and provide feedback about how the communication climate is (or is not) changing. This is not a short-term task, nor necessarily one that will lead to great recognition, but it is one of the most valuable ways in which the internal communicator can add value to the business.

Table 3.3 Positive and negative communication climate

Positive communication climate	Negative communication climate
People trust each other	People are wary of saying what they think; they assume others do not have goodwill towards them
Conflict is resolved openly	Conflict is allowed to fester and/or settled through internal politics
People are willing and keen to share knowledge	Knowledge is power
People have confidence in their ability to communicate	Communication skills are generally poor
Mistakes are accepted as learning opportunities	Mistakes are punished
People feel able to challenge policies and behaviours they disagree with	Dissent is equated with disloyalty
Diversity of opinion, perspective, or personality is welcomed	There is strong pressure to conform
Communicating across departmental and hierarchical barriers is encouraged	People are expected to use approved channels
People believe that managers are interested in their views	People believe that managers are working to a hidden agenda
People help each other formulate and present ideas	People score points off each other
It is usually clear who to talk to about an issue	Responsibilities and areas of expertise/interest are not very transparent
It is OK to admit what you do not know	It is dangerous to admit any weaknesses
People are encouraged and supported in setting up informal networks	The company seeks to control informal communication, and especially the grapevine
Communication competence is a developmental priority	'People wouldn't get to be managers here if they couldn't communicate'
People are encouraged to spend working time on reflection and review	People are driven by task achievement – getting things done
Senior managers provide role models for open communication	Senior managers delegate communication to 'professionals'

Summary

In this chapter, we have expanded the role of internal communication way beyond its traditional remit. From a *provider* of communication it must evolve into a pragmatic *enabler* of communication within the organization.

References

Azzolini, M. C. and Lingle, J. H. (1993). Internal service performance. *Quality*, Vol 32, No. 11.

Buckingham, M. (2001). What a waste. *People Management*, 11 October.

Clutterbuck, D. and Dearlove, D. (1993). *Raising the Profile*. CIPD.

CHAPTER 4

The employee as stakeholder – a crisis of identity

At first sight it may seem strange to include in a book that focuses solely on employee communications, a chapter dealing with stakeholder communications. However, there are two compelling reasons for this. First, whatever the messages and means of communication that are employed to all external (i.e. non-employee) stakeholders, the employee can make or break their impact. A customer ringing a helpline for assistance can detect in the first sentence of a greeting whether or not they are dealing with a 'listening' airline, bank or car rental company. Equally, a shareholder or investment analyst attending a friend's wedding and meeting an executive from a target company can recognize whether or not 'our people are our most important assets'.

Even more important, many modern employees are also wearing a proliferation of other stakeholder 'hats'. They are sometimes shareholders, often customers or users, frequently members of a local community or interest group and even (via elected office) regulators or (via membership) part of the non-governmental organization community. Thus it is more than a truism to say that the corporate message(s) must be consistent and credible across the whole spectrum of audiences. It is no isolated incident that saw a soon to be made redundant worker from Marconi's Poole factory on evening news bulletins complaining that he had been told only weeks previously how well the company was doing. Not only does the proverbial 'left hand' know within minutes what the 'right hand' is doing or being told, but in the case of the employee the left and right hand (and feet) are often identical. This sets up the possibility and (regularly) the probability that individual employees will face a crisis of identity – which stakeholder 'version' do they believe?

In consequence the corporate communication strategy must allow for proper planning and integration across the whole spectrum of audiences. The one community that will soon spot any cracks will be the organization's internal audience. This is particularly true in the case of values. If, for example, the product or corporate brands advertise and promise 'respect for human beings' then poor human resource provision will give this the lie and yield a cynical staff. Employees do not arrive at their workplace each day and hang up their own values on the way in and replace them with their employer's values for the duration of the working day. Instead they take their values into work and expect them to coexist with the internal culture ('the way we do things around here'). If there is too great a gap between the two, the staff will vote with their feet. Even if they stay they will not be party to selling a value that does not match what they see within the organization.

For internal communicators this sets an agenda for stakeholder management and explains why they may need to take a lead in ensuring its effectiveness:

- Help develop the overall core messages/position and obtain top management buy in and commitment to the same.
- Ensure no messages that are inconsistent with overall core messages/position go to any specific stakeholder groups.
- Explore means of inspiring employees to act as (proactive) ambassadors.
- Put in place and regularly review feedback from stakeholders (to ensure employee communication is appropriately meshed/ adapted).

However, even before the internal communicators seek to deal with these tasks, the leadership of the organization must be clear on their strategy – both business and communication. It is easy to state the need for an integrated communication strategy. The question then arises of how to develop a strategy which addresses all groups effectively.

Understanding your stakeholders

For each stakeholder group – from employees to customers, to shareholders – there is in essence a *psychological contract*, which defines the group's expectations of the organization and vice versa. This was referred to in the context of the employee group in the previous chapter.

For each stakeholder group it is critical that the company understands what is expected of it, what it can expect in return, and how important it is that the company meets the expectations of the particular stakeholder group. Groups should be assessed against strategic aims according to three criteria – influence, impact and alignment. For example:

- To what extent will the strategy have a positive or negative effect on them?
- What potential do they have to influence the business directly or indirectly (via other stakeholders), positively or negatively?
- How robust is the business's existing reputation with them?
- How likely is it that the effects of the company's actions towards this group will act as a prompt for action by other groups?
- How far does the strategy align with their existing beliefs about the company's values and purpose?
- How far do they share the company's values and purpose in this area?

What should emerge from this discussion is a view of how the various groups' needs stack up against each other, where they might clash and where they might reinforce each other. All of these can be measured to some extent.

Which stakeholders matter most?

A simple, yet very effective approach to deciding how to respond to different stakeholder groups – particularly when considering the effect of, say, a factory closure or the launch of a new product, is *stakeholder mapping* (Scholes and Johnson, 1998). Stakeholder mapping is built around two dimensions: level of influence and impact (how big an effect the stakeholder group has on the organization's well-being). Analysis of each audience enables the communication team to determine where to place a great deal of effort and where to do no more than make the correct noises. However, quiescent audiences have a habit of bestirring themselves if a strong enough stimulus occurs. This may be very far away from their immediate concerns, but strike the right dischord – for example, the death of young porpoises in fishing nets used to catch fish 10 000 miles away to supply cat food. Moreover, apparently insignificant groups can greatly leverage their impact through alliance or, increasingly, through the intelligent use of technology. It is now possible for a small group of activists to reach tens of millions of a multinational company's customers, by asking people to forward an e-mail to friends and colleagues. It does not need a virus. All it takes is a message sufficiently compelling for people to want to pass it on.

In this battle of reputation, a key weapon is how each stakeholder perceives the company in the first place. If the campaigning message from activists is contrary to their beliefs about the company's values, they are much less likely to continue the chain than if they are already predisposed to believe the claims made. Clearly, the greater the potential of the stakeholder group to influence the success of the business and the higher the business impact of the stakeholders, the more important it is to maintain a constructive dialogue.

That dialogue becomes easier, the greater the alignment of values between the company and the stakeholder group. However, there is another side to the argument – the influence of society itself. It is important to bear in mind that society in general – whether the board likes it or not – will act as an arbiter between each of the stakeholder groups and the company. Society makes judgements about the urgency of dealing with issues. For

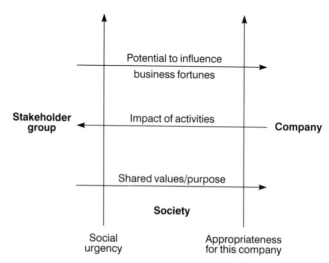

Figure 4.1 Prioritizing stakeholder demands

example, is there a real pressure for getting more women into senior management? Is the UK consumer being asked to pay too much for CDs? The more society judges it appropriate for a company to be involved in a particular issue, the more positive the company's response is likely to be (Figure 4.1). Although society is made up of many interest groups with different agendas, there always exists a dominant consensus that evolves and changes. The dominant consensus will provide (or limit) the business's licence to operate.

Employees, customers and investors: the triumvirate of key stakeholders

For most organizations, the three most influential stakeholders will normally be employees, customers and investors. Company philosophy (and the practicalities of doing business) will normally decide in what order they are ranked. Three discrete disciplines have grown up to address the company's interactions with these audiences: respectively, industrial (and human) relations, customer relationship management (CRM) and investor relations.

'Industrial relations' is a term, which has become heavily imbued with negative associations. Whatever it was, or is, intended to be, it evokes in many people a picture of conflict between workers and management, of attempts to control and manipulate and of the use and abuse of negotiating power. Human Relations was initially seen as a less confrontational approach, but may be gaining a pejorative flavour. Employee relationship management (ERM) is a descendent, several times removed, of industrial relations, more attuned to twenty-first century society.

Customer relationship management is a relatively recent term, which describes a process of maximizing the value of customers to the business through the quality of relationship the company has with them. It can be seen, at one level, as a repackaging of service quality in which technology has made it easier to deliver what many companies already aspired to. Or, at another level, it can be seen as an intelligent attempt to enter a new era of personalized relationships with customers, in which *mutual* value creation becomes the driving force.

Investor relations is a discipline with a single, highly focused objective – maintaining the share price at the highest level possible. It is based in large part on the premise that investors rely less on previous financial track record than on a variety of forward-looking factors (of which past performance is but one), built largely around the level of belief in top management's ability to deliver what it promises.

These three processes, and the communication approaches and media attached to them, rarely if ever meet in most companies. Of the three, the one that has been thought through the most deeply and has made most effective use of the new technologies is CRM. Indeed, a very strong argument can be made for applying the philosophy and approaches of CRM to relationships with both employees and investors, with the aim of creating greater value from both of these relationships, too. The concepts of ERM and investor relationship management (IRM) come directly from this comparison.

Customer relationship management addresses three basic issues:

- the product itself, including attributes such as price and place of delivery
- the systems that support the customer interface – from marketing through delivery, to after-sales
- the customer experience.

Although the first of these is important, most investment in CRM generally addresses the other two issues. Similarly in IRM, the actual company performance is usually outside the influence of the investor relations professional, so that attention is focused on the means of communication. The opposite may often be the case with ERM – companies typically spend more money and effort on the tangibles of the relationship with employees (pay, office accommodation and so on) than on building the intangible relationships that underlie motivation and performance.

However, the principles behind CRM, IRM and ERM are, for the most part very similar, if not identical. In essence, for CRM these are:

1 The psychological contract: clarity about what the customer expects of the organization and vice versa; the consensual agreement as to who does what. This sometimes involves a high level of customer education.
2 Relationship building: the importance of moving from transactional interactions to long-lasting and evolving relationships; the emphasis on mutual benefit.
3 Feedback: continuous improvement and customization of systems as a result of analysing customer behaviour and responses.
4 Integration: bringing together diverse activities so that they all support the building of customer relationships.

As Table 4.1 shows, there are strong parallels in the goals of CRM and ERM.

Similarly, poor publicity about the way the company treats its customers or employees will often have a negative impact on investor sentiment. While investors, large or small, may not be overly concerned as long as they see the profits coming in, they will discount future performance if they perceive that the company is storing up problems that may emerge later in customer or employee behaviour. Equally, investor disquiet may make it more difficult to provide the level of compensation that will attract and retain key management talent – and so the cycle continues.

Table 4.1 Goals of CRM, IRM and ERM

Goals of CRM	Goals of IRM	Goals of ERM
Customer retention/ loyalty	Investor loyalty	Employee loyalty
Customer goodwill	Investor goodwill	Employee goodwill
Ease of doing business	Response to investors' needs for information	More effective teamwork and inter-team work
Customer-driven innovation	Support by investors for investment, acquisition/ divestment and/or for other major changes in the business	Acceptance of change, by employees and employee-led innovation
Cost containment and profit improvement	Growing and maintaining the share price	Improving and managing performance
Reinforcing the corporate/product brand	Maintaining the reputation of the company	Reinforcing the employee brand

Note: These three sets of goals (CRM, IRM and ERM) are inextricably linked, although it is not always obvious to people in the three functional areas. We know from numerous studies over the past twenty years that employee motivation and goodwill have a direct impact on customer experiences and, therefore, on customer goodwill. It is hard for an unhappy or cynical employee to make customers feel welcome. Employees who stay longer tend to have greater experience, which enables them to handle customer problems more effectively and with a greater armoury of responses. Experience in installing call centres, in particular, has amply identified the need for effective interfaces within and between teams, if the customer experience is to be enhanced rather than undermined.

A first step, for professionals in both ERM and IRM, is for the organization to invest in building the same quality of processes or relationship management as are aspired to in CRM. Let us take each of the four CRM principles in turn.

The psychological contract

The psychological contract is referred to many times in this book. Building enduring, trusting relationships requires a continuing effort in information exchange and the creation of *mutual value*. It seems obvious that the more a company focuses on delivering value to its stakeholders, the more loyal they will be, but relationships between many organizations and their stakeholders often become embroiled in arguments about how to share out the pie, rather than how to make it bigger.

A strong and positive psychological contract has a substantial impact on the retention of talent. The seriousness of this problem can be gauged by the fact that surveys suggest that, at any one time, more than one in three people in large companies is thinking about moving on. Yet the introduction of fairly basic communication processes, such as mentoring, that give people an opportunity for dialogue about their personal concerns, can radically change such attitudes. In evaluations of such pro-grammes, where there have been no other significant inter-ventions to distort results, loss of graduate recruits within their first year has plummeted from over 25 per cent to less than 8 per cent, in one case, and loss of more senior people, in a pharmaceutical company, from a similar high to a low of just 2 per cent.

Another issue relating to retention is the simple lack of knowledge of other opportunities the organization provides. If, as a variety of studies suggest, people leave managers, not organizations, then greater awareness of what other functions do and what other jobs entail is likely to increase the proportion of internal moves compared to external moves. **item** is currently exploring web-based solutions that can provide a realistic and readily accessible picture of every job in an organization. A key factor here is to emphasize *what the job is like* rather than *what it does*.

Other practical communication processes for supporting employee retention include:

- staying interviews (lots of companies interview leavers, which helps inform them what they should do less of, but few try to understand why people stay, which helps them understand what they should do more of)

- encouraging the development of virtual teams and support networks
- linking personal development plans more closely to opportunities to gain marketable experience – if someone can get the challenge they need within the organization, why seek it outside? This requires a more sophisticated approach to career self-management than most companies currently employ, but it will become increasingly important as a tool of retention.

Similarly, dialogue with investors about the psychological contract between them and the organization helps build clarity of expectation, which can be highly valuable in times of unexpected performance downturn.

Relationship building

Figure 4.2 illustrates a dilemma common to most companies. Communicating transactions (instructions, task feedback and so on) face to face has been the focus of substantial effort and expense. As a result, although managers vary in their ability to handle this kind of communication, they are relatively comfortable in delivering it. Relational communication (building relationships) is also relatively well developed in the face-to-face context. Transactional communication between remote parties is less effective, but e-mail, by increasing frequency and creating some communication norms, has helped to improve this aspect in recent years. The big hole, for most companies, is remote relational communication – creating goodwill, fellow-feeling, rapport and loyalty among people with whom you have little or no face-to-face interaction.

Effective relationship building in the modern corporation depends on having high capability in all four of these areas. Building a competence across all four areas, both for the

	Transactional	Relational
Face to face	Example: giving verbal instructions	Example: everyday conversations
Remote	Example: giving instructions by e-mail	?

Figure 4.2 Remote relational communication: the black hole?

communication function and for managers across the organization, is essential to maintaining motivation, sense of common purpose and continuous performance improvement. Getting this complicated equation right demands a mixture of systems and behavioural training, along with practical processes to help people recognize in real time where they are succeeding or failing in communicating.

Internal communication functions have a major role to play in helping the organization apply the principles of partnership to what is now in most cases a somewhat coercive activity. Why should people *want* to develop different beliefs, attitudes and behaviours? By developing more effective systems to listen to people and stimulate dialogue, communication functions (in tandem with Human Resources) can help to make culture change a bottom-up process, which is far more powerful and sustainable.

Much the same applies to developing relationships with investors. Trust comes through regular, frequent and personal dialogue. Where the company has numerous small shareholders, different tactics may be required to create opportunities for real dialogue. A shareholder web site, for example, can provide a sense of community among small shareholders, as can regional information events, which overcome the problems of travelling to the statutory shareholder meetings. Given that large shareholders, in particular, are concerned about the competence of the top team as a whole, there is also a case for making one executive director responsible for handling all investor enquiries each month. (It also helps to increase the investor awareness of executives, who would otherwise be insulated from investors!)

One of the subordinate aims of CRM is to make each customer feel like an audience of one – to customize all communication to that person's individual circumstances and needs. Again, this is becoming technically possible and arguably highly desirable within organizations. At present, however, the trend seems to be in the opposite direction – one of the most common complaints about e-mail systems is that people indiscriminately communicate to lists of people, most of whom are not interested. **item** predicts that, within the next three years, many employees will receive their own, customized internal newspaper, refined to compromise between what the organization wants the employee to know and what the employee wishes to find out.

The same should be equally applicable to investors. Although there are regulatory issues to consider, in terms of equal access to price-sensitive information, investor web sites can be equipped with appropriate data links into operational areas of the company, to allow each analyst to build their own, unique view of the organization.

Feedback

Customer feedback is the lifeblood of effective marketing. Of course, companies spend much time and effort on 'listening' processes. But dissatisfaction with tried and tested methods is rapidly increasing.

Large-scale annual, or even longer cycle, employee opinion surveys provide a great deal of one-off data, upon which some forms of remedial action can be based. But they suffer from increasingly obvious weaknesses, among them:

- the cycle of change within businesses is much faster than it was, so the survey data rapidly becomes irrelevant
- questionnaires only elicit responses to questions asked. Many of the most important questions (for employees) do not get asked either because the company does not want to raise expectations, or because the need to compare against other companies obliges them to use standard questions
- comparability of responses within international companies is a nightmare of interpretation, to the extent that some companies are now questioning whether it would be better to carry out more local, culturally adapted surveys
- large, infrequent surveys too easily become part of the routine, like performance appraisals – an exercise to be done as quickly as possible, so managers can get on with the 'real' business of running the company.

An ERM approach focuses feedback processes around specific areas of concern, identified through electronic and telephone sampling of internal audiences on a much more frequent basis. Instead of infrequent, large surveys sent to everyone, it would conduct much more frequent surveys of smaller samples – perhaps as few as 200 people at a time. This enables rapid identification and resolution of problems and creates opportunities to build on people's enthusiasms.

'Testing the temperature' of the organization could even be done on a daily basis. Constant sampling using proven measures such as commitment, trust, supportiveness, motivation would give a broadly accurate picture of the state of the organization at any point in time.

In a similar manner, other institutionalized methods of gaining feedback, such as cascade briefings, need radical overhaul in most organizations, if they are to develop genuine dialogue between the company and its employees. Raising the competence of both managers and their direct reports to engage in dialogue, making information available electronically to support discussion, and encouraging inter-team briefings are all areas in which the internal communication professional can help raise the quality and quantity of useful communication.

From an IRM perspective, gathering feedback is probably one of the most effectively performed tasks of the investor relations function. However, there are many more ways to become informed than are typically used. For example, job-shadowing analysts and brokers, inviting investors other than the company's official brokers to address senior management meetings (or even meetings of middle managers or the sales team), or involving analysts in much broader research projects about the long term future of the industry sector.

Integration

Customer relationship management recognizes the need to integrate all the customer-influencing functions and activities into one seamless system, or as close as possible to it. Yet, as we saw in Chapter 3, 'The internal community of communication', communication inside the business is a tangled mess of responsibilities. Apart from the internal communication function, employees receive information and messages from most other departments, and in particular from Human Resources (usually directly) and marketing (indirectly, because they access customer communication, too). Responsibility for the delivery mechanisms is also split between the communication function and IT, if not more widely.

Tomorrow's communicating company will have to get a grip on this confusion. That does not necessarily mean exerting control, which may not be possible, but it does mean creating frameworks which encourage co-operation between communicating functions, consistency of messages to employees, and rapid sharing and analysis of the implications of employee feedback.

The reality for the next decade is that staff roles that do not integrate will not survive; any function that is not built into the walls of core functions is a natural candidate for outsourcing, or for finding other ways to achieve the same tasks. The threat is also an opportunity – the communication function is sufficiently unthreatening to develop alliances relatively easily within the organization.

The more organizations rely upon extracting maximum value from the interaction between people and IT, the greater the case for ERM. Given that ERM is an integrative activity, the communication function cannot go it alone.

Equally, investor relations is not strengthened by its isolation from the rest of the business. Linking IRM more closely with ERM and CRM will be helpful in a number of ways:

- By identifying and being proactive in dealing with the influence of one area on the other. (For example, would a better understanding by employees of how a large institutional investor decides whether or not to invest in their company change attitudes towards uncomfortable change initiatives?)
- By giving the investor relations function a stronger appreciation of undercurrents in the business, which might influence investor perceptions.
- By giving extra credibility to what top management is saying, through increased contact by investors with customers and employees.

Indeed, all three activities – IRM, ERM and CRM – have much to gain from a more integrated approach.

Setting the strategy

Once the overall business strategy is agreed, the top team and the board need to take the lead in the communication management process by taking responsibility for creating a top-line communication strategy. What that means is making a clear, explicit statement of their intentions – and, just as important, of the core messages which follow from them, indicating where and why the various messages might need to be articulated with different emphases for different groups. The board must become ambassadors for the company's values and intentions towards its stakeholders.

In this way, the top team members – themselves likely to be key deliverers and recipients of communication with all groups – can themselves be more sure they will be holding a consistent line. They will also have prepared a sound basis from which communication specialists can back their efforts with a variety of activities and media, appropriate for particular audiences.

Reporting performance is an important aspect of strategy-related communication to stakeholders. Some boards are now widening the remit of their annual reports – both in print and in face-to-face communication – to put on record their performance in several stakeholder relationships.

If employees and 'loyal' customers are to be seen as stakeholders, how will their 'new' status affect the information they are given? Quite radical changes associated with disclosure and feedback can be anticipated – ask any organization with a large proportion of employee or customer shareholders. It might be considered that the current style of neither the annual report nor employee journal or published business plan is any longer appropriate. Their replacement by *stakeholder reports, journals* and *plans* could be strongly argued.

> Develop the overall core messages position and obtain top management buy-in and commitment to the same.

In principle, if senior management have agreed on business strategy, overall communication strategy and values, the internal communicator's job is simple. In practice it is anything but! The senior team regularly acquiesces rather than commits to this core doctrine.

Part of the internal communicator's job is to ascertain what if anything is 'agreed' – often a case of seeking the lowest common denominator. Some of this information can be obtained if the senior internal communicator participates in the top team's strategy sessions. However, this is not always possible and interviews with members of the top team must be used to fill the gap. If such interviews are 'touchy' a neutral template can be employed. It also helps to get the members of the top team to self-complete such a template before the interview.

Do not be mislead by the individual (be he or she a chief executive, finance or HR director) who says 'all my colleagues agree with me that . . .'. Often they are the least sensitive to the nuances around agreements. Employees can spot such differences a mile off. A hesitation before confirming the top team is united behind the 'new' strategy can deliver more messages than appear in the script itself.

Having established what core agreement there is among the top team (and as a by-product some of the differences), the internal communicator must make a crucial judgement. Has he or she enough to make a pitch for the hearts and minds of employees (and for that matter other external stakeholders)? If not then that message needs to be fed back to the top team. This is high risk and can be career limiting. Before embarking on such a course it is worth bolstering the arguments. Often previous measurement, e.g. employee attitude surveys, communication audits or focus group findings, can provide valuable ammunition. If none are to hand then a 'quick and dirty' check of a sample of employees can ascertain their current view of where the company is heading. If time and issues of confidentiality allow, the 'new' agreed messages can be tested with some sample recipients. One biotech company (about to embark on a full cascade programme) tested their new strategy on a pilot group who in turn could act as communication champions. In the final analysis if the internal communicator feels that the core messages are inadequate then he or she must say so.

If they are adequate or better, then the task is to craft them into a clear and persuasive whole that can be packaged and distributed and supported through all the available channels. A highly visible (and to some apparently trivial) example of this occurs when an organization has launched a new logo or identity. This sometimes follows on a merger where the message can be particularly sensitive. When Glaxo Wellcome merged with SmithKline Beecham the merger was on–off for over a year and there was much uncertainty. The identity for the new company (gsk) was meant to signal a merger of equals (a point of debate both before and after the merger). Irrespective of its effectiveness it was a fact that the day following the merger even the oldest offices in the group were proudly flying the new company flags. Less than a mile away, a high-tech company that also launched a new brand took months to replace existing signage on their head office – indeed, many months later there remained a relic of the old name – a 30-foot banner sign on one main frontage. The look and feel of internal publications, whether in e-formats or printed, are similar trigger points.

Another feature of communicating changed core messages is that the messages may be simple or capable of distillation into two or three simple propositions. The implications are rarely simple and part of the internal communicator's task is to anticipate the myriad of questions and formulate answers. In many instances the top team may not have thought through some of the implications. (In one case a company announced the intention to partially float one of its major subsidiaries. At the same time it raised the prospect of share options for senior executives in the subsidiary. Leaving aside the question of the impact on the non-recipients of options both in the subsidiary and in the rest of the group, the top team concerned failed to consider what would happen if the flotation were pulled after a deterioration in market conditions.)

When messages and accompanying questions and answers are clarified, the internal communicator must feed back to the top team as a whole and ensure maximum commitment to the whole package. This is a step that is often skimped by members of the top team themselves. It is as if they feel they have done their bit by agreeing the overall strategies in the first place and need not concern themselves with the communication to a wider audience. However, they are a crucial ingredient in this mix and must be on board from the start. Devices for cultivating their attention include interviews with each to be published in internal publications giving their personal take on what it all means and/or rotas for face-to-face or online (via chat rooms) questions and answers from staff.

Ensure no messages go to any specific stakeholder groups that are inconsistent with overall core messages/ position.

This is generally not a direct function of the internal communicator. Nevertheless he or she must seek to keep informed of and influence messages prepared for other external stakeholder groups. An annual report or briefing to city analysts that lauds the most recent cost cuts and hints at more to come will not square well with reassuring statements to employees that no more cuts are envisaged. This is not simply a question of style; it is also about content. Because of the rise of openness and the availability of much more information, employees (like other stakeholders) will be able to access reviews and reports that many top team members will never see or read.

Keeping informed involves more than ensuring inclusion on the mailing list for cuttings, press releases and city announcements. It is also about regular face-to-face contact with those in the organization tasked with other communications (e.g. investor relations, regulatory contacts, corporate counsel, health and safety, etc.). One model process involves a regular meeting of such interested parties (preferably under the auspices of the CEO) to review upcoming events and issues. This is often considered in the case of one off projects such as mergers (e.g. the gsk merger involved a joint communications team formed from the two component companies that published a regular merger newsletter for staff) but not as an ongoing process.

Explore means of inspiring employees to act as (proactive) ambassadors

At the start of this chapter the point was made that an employee (any employee) can make or break the impression that the organization is seeking to give to its external stakeholders. It is therefore important to elicit the employee's assistance and commitment in this task. This is primarily a matter of motivation. Employees need to feel good about their organization before they will willingly act as ambassadors (unwilling employees represent a cross between Trappist monks and hostages). Making them feel good includes having a clear notion of what they are doing in the organization, being valued for this and being clear about where their work contributes to the overall strategy. All these are part of the internal communicator's normal tasks (even if they achieve these through the work and behaviour of others).

However, good ambassadors need also to have the support of the organization behind them. They need to know something about the organization over and above their own roles. What do others do? What are the basic building blocks and processes? Even if they did not need this information in order to be effective in their own roles, they will need it to be effective ambassadors (e.g. Unilever discovered mercury at a plant in the subcontinent. While not the source, they paid for the decontamination and even Greenpeace were minded to compliment the company on the way the incident was handled. Such stories are not only of interest to employees but vital in rebutting the thought that all global companies are the same.)

Notice that the references are to employees and not solely to managers. All employees will find themselves in situations where they can behave as ambassadors and, therefore, they all need access to such information – the final nail in the coffin of those who argue that 'need to know' rules. In addition to information, some potential ambassadors may justify greater investment and resource. And here the main emphasis is probably on managers and others who will have occasion to give talks or presentations both within and without the organization. Support materials, e.g. slides and handouts, can be conveniently stored and updated on the organization's intranets. Regular newsletters or selected press cuttings can be circulated. Training in communication skills may also be relevant to a much wider group than previously thought necessary.

> Put in place and regularly review feedback from stake-holders (to ensure employee communication is appropriately meshed/adapted).

As with all communication plans the measurement of outcomes and the gathering of feedback are essential. 'If you cannot measure it you cannot manage it' remains as fundamental to communication as to other management disciplines. In the case of communication it is probably a more fast-moving process. Feedback from team briefings often fails to be effective because the information takes too long to percolate back up the chain, and the urgency to act and remedy issues dissipates or, at best, the actions appear ponderous.

Stakeholder communication and the four pillars of communication

Like every other communication activity, managing relationships with stakeholders can be enhanced greatly by:

- clarity of purpose
- appropriate communication behaviours by top management
- building trusting interfaces
- effective processes for sharing information.

In practical terms, the organization needs to invest significant effort in listening to stakeholders, understanding their goals and attempting wherever possible to explain the organization's objectives against that background. One common example concerns corporate investment in community involvement. For example, in a special anniversary year the UK retailer WH Smith promised staff that they would match pound for pound the funds raised by the staff in support of a project by the charity of the staff's choice.

Even where there is little or no opportunity for alignment of objectives, there may be room for some alignment of values. If that, too, is not possible, then the company can at least earn respect for being open and honest about what it aims to achieve and why. The clearer you are about your motives and objectives, the less likely people will be to ascribe less worthy or less reputable ones to you!

Top management's role here is vital. In a recent case, the CEO and another top team member of Consignia, the UK state-owned postal service were awarded a pay increase at the same time the organization was negotiating drastic cuts in the workforce. The pay rises were more than most individual employees earned in total. Only swift action by the executives concerned, in foregoing their increases, avoided severe damage to the organization's reputation, not just among employees, but among customers, who had also been informed that their second daily post could be cut.

The lives top managers lead and the values they demonstrate are critical elements in managing corporate reputation with stakeholders. How can you portray a company as environmentally concerned, if its leaders drive gas-guzzling cars, for example? How can the company claim to be socially aware if all its top team are from one, dominant social group?

The most important behaviours the top team can demonstrate, however, are a genuine willingness to listen to and a desire to understand each of the key stakeholder audiences. With mutual respect comes the opportunity to disagree cordially; to engage in dialogue not conflict.

This, too, is the core of building trusting interfaces with stakeholders. Without continuous dialogue, there is no trust. It also helps, however, to build trust through association; that is, to ensure that groups with whom the organization does have a strong bond of trust should be encouraged and assisted to talk to those who are more suspicious. The first instinct of managers is often that this is a highly dangerous thing to do. What if those with negative attitudes influence the positives? Yet, as we have already discussed, it is getting easier and easier for stakeholders to communicate with each other and for people to be members of several stakeholder groups with different interests and perspectives.

Those few companies, which have tried to bring together different stakeholder groups in a mutual 'learning community' have normally found the approach to be highly beneficial, both in terms of increasing their own sensitivity to issues and building understanding among stakeholders. For example, see the Shell case study at the end of this chapter.

The employees' role in such dialogue is pivotal. As a young journalist, one of the authors had a habit of getting 'lost' on organized press visits. Finding opportunities to listen unsupervised to ordinary employees frequently put the story being promoted by the company into a different perspective. Similarly, an experienced analyst in London's financial centre explains: 'When I hear things from the CEO, I discount it. When I receive the same message from employees as well, I'm far more impressed.' If a company is, for example, going through a major culture change and/or restructuring, inviting employees to the annual general meeting provides an opportunity for investors large and small to hear informally what is happening on the ground. Even if there are problems, the greater alignment of message between the top and the rank and file, the more believable the business message will be.

The consequences of *not* achieving trust with the internal stakeholders in general are dealt with in other chapters. With regard to the business's reputation with other stakeholders, however, they are more severe than companies typically acknowledge. Every interaction between a supplier, customer, member of the press, or financial intermediary and the employees either reinforces or undermines the brand personality top management wants to project and the credibility of the business and its leaders in terms of future delivery on promises. Cumulatively, these many small encounters have a substantial impact on every strategically critical aspect of the company' operations.

Openness of information is also a key factor in developing partnerships with stakeholders. We can see the underlying problem in the frequently confusing attempts by western democracies to steer a path between freedom of information and official secrecy. No sooner is there a legislative or procedural move to open up more official documentation and process to public scrutiny, than it is countered by new restrictions on anything that might be embarrassing to the government of the day. The intellectual desire to be open is frequently overcome by the emotional need for security and control of the environment. Information management becomes in large part a process of 'official' leaks with a positive spin, countered by 'unofficial' leaks, which present a less positive picture.

True openness of information starts from the premises that:

- very little information truly needs to be kept secret. Information, which is used against the company, tends in most cases to be only a part of a bigger picture. The more information available, and the more clearly it is related to the big picture, the more difficult for it to be misused
- sharing information, even if it has been very expensive to gather, is usually better than closeting it, because it results in a return flow of ideas, critiques and other reciprocal contributions
- information that people worry about (for example, personal files kept on them) becomes of marginal interest once they know they can inspect it. (When US data privacy laws first began to bite, some companies invested heavily in resources to deal with floods of enquiries from employees, who wanted to review the records held on them. Very, very few people bothered.) Secrecy creates suspicion
- ease of access makes people more selective about what information they seek
- employees can usually be trusted with information of high sensitivity. (When British Aerospace's Military Aircraft Division published its detailed business plan to all employees, there were fears that it would be leaked widely. The opposite was the case – employees (even those who were made redundant not long after) showed remarkable common sense and loyalty, as a result of the trust placed in them.)
- secrecy encourages malpractice. There is a clear correlation between 'corporate deviance' (behaviours such as operating a cartel or burying information about product safety) and the existence of a culture of secrecy.

When considering how to build openness with stakeholders, the internal communicator should consider the following:

- To what extent can internally focused publications be circulated to other audiences, such as the City, or the press? (If they can be left in reception for visitors to read, there's not much point in keeping them secret!)

- What is the boundary between information available on the Internet and the company intranet? While security reasons will usually prevent full open access to the intranet, much of the information on one can readily be transferred to the other.
- Are we prepared to establish hyperlinks between our web site and those of organizations, which represent other stakeholder interests? (For example, a pharmaceutical company might direct web enquiries for information to the sites of a medical charity or patient support group which has a useful library.)
- Can we instigate and support conferences and symposia, where the views expressed may be very different to those the company wishes to promote?
- Are we willing to open up in-company events to outsiders. (For example, IBM has for years financed places at training events for participants from charities.)
- Can we open up internal discussion networks to external stakeholders, to inject a different set of views and to expose them to the views of our employees?

The key to success here is an attitude shift that welcomes the sharing of information and eschews the opportunity to manipulate it. Here, perhaps, is one of the core distinctions between internal communication and public relations. Whereas the latter is primarily about selective sharing, the former is (or should be) more about the encouragement of open sharing.

Summary

Building strong and positive relationships with stakeholders outside the company depends heavily upon the quality of relationships with internal stakeholders. Companies must recognize that the boundaries between these two sets of audiences are becoming increasingly porous. Establishing policies and practices that use open communication to build partnerships with stakeholders should be a priority within the business planning process.

Case study

Developing stakeholder relationships at Shell

The climate for multinationals is changing, particularly for companies involved in activities that are seen to threaten the environment and the sustainability of natural resources. Increasingly the role of business in society and the magnitude of its social and environmental responsibilities are being questioned. Companies are faced with new expectations from investors, competitors and other stakeholders. Shell began to realize these changes in society when they were taken by surprise in 1995, facing strong opposition to its planned disposal of the Brent Spar oil storage buoy in the North Sea and long periods of protest in Nigeria surrounding the execution of Ken Saro-Wiwa and fellow Ogoni tribal leaders. In the wake of these crises Shell was ready to learn from experience and began a worldwide programme of engagement with different stakeholder groups to try to understand more fully society's expectation of multinational companies, in particular the energy industry, and to adopt a new policy of communicating its principles and policies and its commitment to openness and transparency about its activities and their impact on society.

'Discovering the knowledge gap' – changing the quality of relationships

Shell realized that the success of its businesses relied on developing a clear understanding of its relationships with others in the world in which they operate. In 1995 the Royal Dutch/Shell Group of companies embarked on a process to better understand the Group's stakeholders, their attitudes and needs and then use the information to develop a new strategy of engagement.

In 1996 the Society's Changing Expectations project was launched, concerned with obtaining views of the ways in which society's expectations of large multinational companies were changing and might be expected to change in the future. It provided an opportunity for Shell to listen to its stakeholders' expectations, through a series of round tables, interviews and surveys among general publics, special publics and Shell managers and employees. The programme combined market research with:

- a review of sixty existing research programmes in twenty-one countries
- intensive internal interviews and analysis with forty-four senior Shell executives
- consultation with Shell graduate recruiters about the views of young people
- a benchmarking survey of practices in twenty-three peer companies
- round-table meetings in fourteen countries, where 159 Shell executives came face-to-face with 145 representatives of special public groups.

Following on from the Society's Changing Expectations project a global reputation research survey was conducted by MORI in 1997, and the results provided a key influence in the development of Shell's communication strategy. The aim of the MORI research was to establish baselines of key expectations towards Shell; Shell's position versus other companies – criteria for judging companies' performance and reputation; and a detailed analysis of Shell's image. The research covered:

- 7551 interviews with members of the general public in ten countries
- 1288 interviews with special publics in twenty-five countries, which include academics, business leaders, investment fund managers, pressure groups, influential religious leaders, representatives of government and non-governmental organizations, and journalists
- 583 questionnaires to senior Shell managers from fifty-five countries.

The research showed that Shell's economic contribution to society, technology leadership and product quality were positively recognized, but on the other two legs of sustainable development, i.e. social and environmental, Shell was rated poorly by both the general public and opinion leaders. These findings revealed a clear gap between Shell's perception of its business and those of wider society, but they also pointed towards a response: a commitment to greater engagement and dialogue to close this 'knowledge gap'.

'Creating a human face' – listening to our stakeholders

The first step in Shell's new relationship with stakeholders was to revise its Statement of General Business Principles, first written and published in 1976. New sections were included on human rights and sustainable development, and the need to be open and accountable – to consult, communicate and listen – was enshrined as a core business principle. In addition mandatory Health, Safety and Environment Policy and Procedures were set up.

To enhance greater understanding of Shell's revised business principles and activities the Shell Report was created, demonstrating the company's progress in living up to its commitments, its business principles and in meeting the expectations of its stakeholders. The Shell Report provides a consolidated view of the Group's activities and impacts across the three strands of sustainable development: economic, environmental and social. The data in the Shell Report has been increasingly verified over time and the verification process is now one of the largest conducted by a company. In addition the Shell Report invites stakeholders to tell Shell what they think of its performance, issues and dilemmas stimulating a global debate about the role and responsibilities of business. Besides external stakeholders, the Shell Report is distributed each year to all employees accompanied by a letter from the chairman.

Shell also created an external web site in November 1996, offering access to all aspects of the company's performance and communications, including the issues raised and assessed in the **Shell Report**. *The web site offers an opportunity for stakeholders to respond to Shell, through e-mailing comments and questions to 'Tell Shell' or directly posting views onto the uncensored open forum on the web site.*

Employees are encouraged to 'Tell Shell' through the intranet, which is a central medium of internal communication within Shell. They can also express their views about particular issues and performance progress in the organization through the Shell People Survey that takes place every two years. This is a way to continue the dialogue between leadership and staff. The results and progress updates are published on the intranet.

The 'listening and responding' approach is about communicating Shell's commitment to its business principles and involving stake-holders in its policy making process. It involves different levels of interaction and channels of communication both with internal and external stakeholders.

For the most part, externally it has taken the form of regular face-to-face meetings with a wide range of stakeholder representatives, including Shell's sternest critics: these meetings range from information updates on the company's activities, to consultation about specific issues and planned activities. These private sessions have been matched by making a very public commitment to listen and respond. An above and below the line communications programme – using advertising, forums, mailings, media relations and the web site – was created to inform people globally about the ways in which Shell conducts its business and its commitment to the principles of sustainable develop-ment. It seeks to start a debate with opinion formers – each advertisement ends with a request to Shell's stakeholders to 'talk to us and let us know what you think. We promise to listen and respond to your views'. All these activities prepare the ground for further communication and facilitate the establishment of a relationship with key opinion formers.

Shell staff are crucially important to this dialogue, both as part of the audience as well as external ambassadors. An internal 'listening and responding' tool kit has been presented at workshops around the world with staff from the different businesses and operating units, to encourage country managers to create their own stakeholder dialogue and develop above and below the line communications programmes adapted to suit the needs of their local markets.

'Action on the ground' – building constructive relationships

Around the world Shell has embarked on building relationships with local communities, non-governmental organization and government institutions. Some of the more recent projects include Shell Philippines Exploration in Malampaya, the Athabasca Oil Sands project in Canada and the Camisea project in Peru. Engaging in consultation forums provides an opportunity for different stakeholders to come together and discuss social and environmental issues that need to be addressed. The Malampaya project, operated by Shell Philippines Exploration (SPEX), extracts and processes gas from deep below the sea and pipes it over 500 km to onshore power plants. It will enable the Philippines to reduce dependency on imported fuels. Detailed social and environmental studies were conducted and stakeholders consulted before construction. This led to the rerouting of the pipeline to avoid environmental and culturally sensitive areas.

Several development programmes were initiated in partnership with others. For example SPEX set up a partnership with Pilipinas Shell Foundation, a non-government organization specializing in developing skills, to stimulate local enterprise. A fish farm set up under the programme is already providing enough milkfish to pay back its initial investment within six months. Likewise SPEX is helping to improve health care by sharing its emergency medical treatment facilities with the local community. To oversee its activities, SPEX has established a Sustainable Development Council that includes people from outside Shell.

This approach to assessing the social and environmental impacts is a core element of any new project. No investment proposal is passed without a review of the sustainable development implications.

The Athabasca Oil Sands project, set up by Shell Canada and its joint ventures, involves the mining of oil from sands in northern Alberta. New techniques have reduced the costs and environmental impacts of mining oil sands. The project includes new environmental design features and stakeholder consultation. Government, local communities and local first nations are, and will continue to be active partners in the project through consultations, partnerships and community pro-grammes. Shell has set up an independent panel made up of representatives of local communities and environmental organizations to help ensure that Shell meets its climate change commitments on this project.

Building relationships is about facilitating dialogue and building trust. It is about listening and responding, but also about learning from experience, and continuing to move forward. The Camisea project provides such an example. Camisea, in the Lower Urubamba region of the upper Amazon in the Peruvian rainforest contains two large fields of natural gas and condensate. Developing these gas reserves called for a high level of interaction between staff employees and external stakeholders. Around 250 stakeholders were engaged to give help and advice, ranging from international non-governmental organizations to community liaison officers.

In the appraisal phase, in consultation with the local community, Shell decided not to build access roads, which would have opened up a hitherto undisturbed area. Instead, all the material, including the drilling rig, was brought in by barge, hovercraft and helicopter. Because of the perceived risk that diseases could be introduced into the community the operation was run as if it were an offshore platform, with severe site access restrictions and health passports for all workers and visitors.

Even though the project ended in 1998, because the company was unable to reach an agreement on the project terms with the Peruvian government, the project was officially recognized for its work with an award from the International Association of Impact Assessment. The project provided community relations guidelines that are now in place and applied in various degrees in all projects around the world.

Improving the company's communication with stakeholders and building its relationships involves an integrated strategy of creating awareness about its principles and activities, encouraging its audience to engage in dialogue, creating new channels of listening and responding to its stakeholders and working in partnership with them on the ground.

References

Scholes, K. and Johnson, G. (1998). Exploring Corporate Strategy. Prentice Hall.

CHAPTER 5

Vision and values: mirage and sentiment?

A careful mining of the reams of literature on vision and values programmes within organizations reveals a number of largely unpalatable truths, including the following:

- No matter how enthused people are at a corporate event, it does not take long for them to forget.
- Changing the vision and values statements does not change the culture.
- Getting people to *care* about the vision and values at anything but the most superficial level is extremely difficult.

The vogue for vision and values was at its strongest in the 1980s, as one of the trappings of the business excellence movement. But companies still feel that they should both have and try to live up to what we now sometimes refer to as their V2.

In theory, making people aware of what the company aims to become (its ambitions and desired characteristics) and the values (the fundamental principles and behaviours expected to help it achieve them) should line people up behind common objectives, inspire them to renewed efforts and provide a touchstone for difficult decisions. In practice, the entropic tendencies of people and organizations to ignore exhortations and generally go their own way tend to make it all a lot more difficult.

It helps to be clear at the beginning as to what we mean by V2. The simple answer is that vision statements are descriptions of what and where the company wants to be in a more or less defined time frame, usually at least five years into the future. The vision has to be meaningful to those it is intended to influence. Effective visions in business are dreams that have sufficient contact with reality and desirable outcomes to galvanize many people to action.

Values statements attempt to capture the core principles, which the company will apply in getting there. A typical values statement of the 1980s would contain a list of stakeholders and how the company should behave towards each of them. Values statements of the 1990s tend to be built around a series of key words, such as teamwork, integrity or service.

The issue becomes more complicated when we ask 'whose vision and values?' Top management's view of the world is unlikely to be the same as that of people at middle management levels. It will have even less in common with that of people at operator level. Although most organizations talk about 'our vision', this assumption of inclusiveness is little more than an assumption. To be inclusive a vision and values need to engage people in both intellectual understanding and emotional commitment. That inevitably means that the vision and values must recognize (or change) people's current understanding of the role and potential of the business, and recognize the importance and relevance of the values – both individual and cultural – that people bring with them.

How do you arrive at the right vision and values in the first place?

It is not enough just to have a set of vision and values. They have to have a discernible impact on the business. A variety of studies in the late 1980s and early 1990s (Campbell, Devine and Young, 1990) looked at the nature of values statements. The common findings were that most were uninspiring, largely irrelevant to the audiences they were aimed at and depressingly similar in their wording.

To be genuinely impactful a value set needs to be:

1 *Relevant*: people have to be able to see how it makes a difference and why it is important to the business, to their team and to themselves. In practice, relevance operates in the reverse order – the further the impact of the value is from the personal, the less commitment and urgency the individual will feel towards it.

Vague statements like 'To be the best' or 'Teamwork' are unlikely to have any lasting motivational effect on the majority of employees. Key questions to tell the relevance are:
(a) Why is it important to the business? My team? Me?
(b) How will I recognize the difference?

2 *Credible*: the work of Collins and Porras (2000) in the USA and our own review of high performance companies (Goldsmith and Clutterbuck, 1998) suggest on the one hand that very specific highly ambitious visions can be powerful motivators for change. Aligning senior managers behind big goals results in their becoming role models for others in the organization.

Yet ambitious visions can equally evoke disbelief, cynicism and worse. Big goals, out of reach and emotional or practical experience of the employees, can just as easily be too remote to influence people's day-to-day behaviour.

The moderating factor in establishing credibility appears to be the perception by employees and others that the process is already underway, albeit there is a long way to go. The couch potato who says 'I'm going to walk 30 miles tomorrow' only becomes credible when he or she has set off on the journey.

The effective vision and values, therefore, is a combination of both *words and demonstrable actions*. It is about what has already been achieved towards the goal as much as what is aspired to.

3 *Understandable*: the most powerful vision statements are often those that sum up aspirations in a single phrase. For example, the vision of the Japanese operations of Amersham Pharmacia Biotech is simply 'Make customers' dreams come true'.

4 *Biased to action*: what does it make people do differently? If it is not personally demanding and aspirational, it probably misses the point. But people have to be able to see immediate steps they can take to achieve the vision and make the values real. The more the big goals can be broken down into short-term steps, achievable with a quantifiable amount of effort, the more people are likely to use the vision and values as a vehicle for personal and group change. A bias for action also demands that the vision instil a sense of urgency. Why change now if there is no pressing need?

5 *Differentiating*: our recent book *Doing it Different* (Clutterbuck and Kernaghan, 1999) looks in detail at how 'whacky' companies around the world survive and thrive on refusing to follow the herd. Among its conclusions is that enduring differences, that bring long-lived competitive advantage, are the product of a business *philosophy*. A philosophy is usually more deeply ingrained than a set of values statements, because it represents strongly held beliefs about the purpose and nature

of the business. Companies with deeply differentiating phi-losophies include WL Gore, Virgin, Dyson, Semco and Ben & Jerry's and other more or less well-known names.

In each case, the founder's or founders' deep-seated beliefs are the starting point, against which all major decisions are made. This often radical difference of perspective leads to many radical differences in approach, making the business appear even more innovative (or whacky). Businesses differ-entiated in this way attract employees and customers because of their philosophy, even when it is not written down.

How communication supports V2

It is obvious that people cannot make use of V2, if they do not know about it. But there is a big difference between knowing about something and knowing it, between knowing and under-standing, and between understanding and applying knowledge constructively. For most organizations, the retention factor – how much people can recall – is low even at the simple level of recognizing what its V2 is. The simplest test, of course, is to ask employees without warning to explain what it says. While retention can be relatively good for a few months after an initial introduction campaign, it typically declines rapidly. One of the main reasons this is so, is that there is no continuing obvious link between the V2 and what happens day-to-day in the business.

V2 and clarity of purpose

In theory, V2 is all about gaining clarity of purpose. The dream should capture the imagination of everyone and focus their efforts. The problem is that clarity declines as reality creeps in. In the heyday of its most successful years, the UK shoemakers Clark's related every decision of any consequence – and many of small consequence – to the question 'But does it sell shoes?' The principal is a valuable one. To make a vision meaningful and actionable, it must be translated into a few, powerful questions, which can be asked continuously and long-term. In essence, the sum of these questions is 'How does this help us achieve the vision?'

We sometimes call these questions lodestar questions, because of their critical guiding role in decision-making. But lodestars have a secondary use beyond acting as a guide. They are also visible, constant reminders of the dream.

Some other examples of lodestar questions used in organiza-tions we have worked with are:

- Will this make our customer come back?
- Would I feel good about explaining this to my kids?
- If we do this, will we do it better than anyone else?
- Can we launch this new product faster than our competitors?
- Will it enhance our reputation as experts?

Relating business decisions to the lodestar questions at meetings and in company news-sheets, for example, is generally more effective than reiterating the V2 itself, because people can see the practical relevance. The V2 becomes assimilated into the collective consciousness most efficiently through frequent observation of how it is applied, not by constant exhortation.

A major problem for many companies, however, is that they have, in addition to V2, a competing set of brand values. We discuss this further in Chapter 7, but it is obvious to an outside observer when an organization is suffering from values confusion. The communication function has a share responsibility for ensuring that the organization has just one vision and one set of values.

V2 and top management behaviour

It is often forgotten that the best statements are not textual (i.e. actions speak louder than words). A planned programme of activities to demonstrate top management commitment to the values can deliver far more punch than any expenditure or videos, booklets, road shows or plastic cards. Inguar Kamprad, founder of IKEA, reinforces the value of thrift by taking the bus to business meetings and always flying back. Liisa Jorenen of SOL emphasizes equality by refusing all of the trappings of an executive, including a secretary. They do so, because they know that they need to be twice as vigilant as any one else in applying core values if those values are to have any credibility or motivational effect on other people.

V2 and information sharing

Rolling out an information campaign may be the most common method of communicating V2, but it is not the most effective according to members of ASPIC. After the initial awareness must come opportunities to relate V2 to every significant aspect of the business. This means, in effect, a substantial process of questioning what is done and why, at all levels, so that people internalize the knowledge. Good practice and wider thinking are an inevitable outcome of this approach.

Repeating the exercise from time to time (say every two years) provides a reminder of V2 and reinforces the concepts in people's minds. Some companies have begun to incorporate this approach with the idea of zero-base management – looking at every system and activity in the business in the light of how it contributes to the vision and whether it is being managed in accordance with the values. Our view is that this will in due course become a commonplace management activity, in which the communication function takes partial responsibility for engaging employees in the process and sharing what has been learned. Consulting staff for their views on how well the organization is sticking to its values and how progress is being made towards the vision is a powerful driver for change.

V2 and trusting interfaces

Many values statements will explicitly or implicitly require behaviours that support teamwork and respect for colleagues. But fulfilment of the vision is also likely to be dependent on the quality of interaction between people and functions. One place where this comes to the fore is the issue of valuing other interpretations of V2 within the organization.

In an international organization, particularly, diversity of perspective and culture is potentially as valuable a characteristic as uniformity of vision and values. When these two apparent opposites are reconciled, they provide a remarkable engine for achievement. Companies are increasingly learning that cultural cloning leads to insufficient internal challenge and higher barriers to innovation. Universal values are a chimera – different cultures place subtly different meanings upon the same words and concepts, which can lead either to significant differences in behaviour, or to resentment against 'cultural imperialism' by the company's country of origin.

Again, in practice some companies have been very effective in balancing the need for consistency with the need for local autonomy. They provide a framework of values, reliant less on worthy words than on broad behaviours, and encourage local operations to interpret them in their own way.

Managing these interfaces is one of the greatest communication challenges for an organization. Too much autonomy in interpretation and the company can be undermined by inappropriate behaviours in isolated subsidiaries. Too little autonomy in interpretation and it becomes difficult for people to relate V2 to their own circumstances and business dilemmas. Stimulating frequent global dialogue on the interpretation of V2 and

publicizing examples of good practice is the minimum requirement in our view, but few companies actively manage this kind
of interchange.

How the IC function can make a difference

The IC function can make a difference in several ways. Among
them:

1 *Helping management clarify the relationship between vision, values
   and brand.*
   (a) Vision = what we aim to *become*.
   (b) Values = how we intend to behave and the beliefs that
       drive our behaviour.
   (c) Brand = the personality and reputation of the enterprise.
       (see Chapter 7 for more in-depth discussion)
2 *Relating major change and minor achievements to the vision and
   values.* Anecdote and parable are among the most powerful
   forms of achieving understanding, attitude change and behaviour change. The power of story is magnified when it contains
   a moral. For example, if innovation is a core value, then it
   should be reflected in the widest range of corporate media,
   from the employee newspaper and e-zines, to the agenda for
   all project or team meetings. And if the vision is to be a global
   player, then each small step can be communicated in the
   context of the longer journey.
      The power of the vision and values comes from their
   continuous use in shaping everyday discussions and actions. A
   one-off campaign achieves little compared with the constant
   flow of small reminders.
3 *Establishing the channels to identify behaviour that undermines the
   vision and values.* Discussion forums, whistle-blowing policies
   that protect people who speak out and surveys that elicit
   employers perception of actual versus desired behaviours by
   themselves and others – there are numerous ways to obtain
   feedback on the reality of how the values are being put into
   practice. Presenting this data to top management helps them
   focus on where to place more effort in bringing about
   change.
4 *Encouraging constructive challenge to the vision and values.* Well-
   founded faith, be it religious or in a corporate future, may be
   strengthened by being tested. *Blind* faith, on the other hand can
   easily be shattered by exposure to reality. One organization we
   encountered holds an annual competition to reward the best
   essay dissenting from corporate policy. The judges are a

mixture of non-executive directors and invited outsiders. The result of this courageous policy is that issues of concern are regularly aired, stimulating debate throughout the organization. It also gives top management an opportunity to explain why particular policies have been adopted and how these support (or are intended to support) the vision and values, in particular from an ethical point of view.

Summary

To prevent vision and values becoming a turn-off to employees and achieving the opposite impact to that intended by top management, the IC function needs to become much more involved in clarifying how to achieve *sustained* employee buy-in. Just as the health of a human body depends on an alert immune system, frequently recharged by testing, the IC function maintains effectiveness of the vision and values system by helping keep it in constant use.

Case study

BSkyB

When a company the size of BSkyB wants to implement change it takes time, planning and courage to devise and construct feasible ideas that will make a difference.

'Living the vision' was the brainchild of incoming Managing Director, Tony Ball, and built around the CRM programme he introduced. The objective of the programme was to identify what needed to change and how best to resolve it.

BSkyB wanted to deliver world-beating customer service that would be embraced by employees around the entire UK workforce. To help them understand the company's customer service vision of providing such a service – employees needed to appreciate:

1 *Awareness*
   (a) *what Sky CRM is aiming to achieve*
   (b) *why Sky has to change*
   (c) *how Sky CRM impacts their department*
   (d) *what the change means for them and their role in the transition.*
2 *Buy-in*
   (a) *co-operate and share information*
   (b) *volunteer their time*

(c) advocate the change

(d) communicate messages that support the change

(e) prepare themselves for a new way of working.

3 Ownership

(a) behave in a way that delivers world-beating customer service.

The audience

Everyone employed by BSkyB would see the material – from people at headquarters to field agents to contact centre staff. A list was drawn up to explain the importance of employees, and the need to see the material. It included:

- Contact centre staff and installers: these people have direct customer contact and the technology and process changes effect them the most.
- Managers: these people have to understand and role-model the new behaviours as well as be champions of the programme.
- Support and professional people: The need to help them understand how world beating customer service includes internal as well as external customers.

Training

To communicate vision, cultural characteristics, strategy, values and dealing with change people were given the opportunity to share their thoughts on Sky's current culture before embarking on a journey into the unknown.

Training days were communicated under the banner of 'living the vision' and were always held at a non-BSkyB site, ensuring that an open-minded and informal environment was created.

- Breaking with tradition: employees spend three days having fun from confidence-building, role-playing, discussing self-awareness and becoming engaged as individuals and learning to believe that their contribution made Sky a great place to work.

Sky speakers

A team of communicators was also nominated and established through all areas of the business to help cascade key messages across all shifts and locations. Monthly meetings were held to brief employees on business and CRM issues, answer their questions and gather feedback from around the company.

Targets

To target specific audiences, taking into account their shift and location they tailored information using the most appropriate medium.

- Face-to-face: *importance was placed on face-to-face communication because the programme requires a high degree of personal change. Cascading the vision and developing a 'teachable point of view' that equipped senior managers to own the vision, and make it personal so they could explain it to their teams, were important elements of the campaign. These elements were introduced through interactive workshops designed to get maximum participation. In addition, presentation cascades, where a team leader was given material to show to their team, proved very popular and 'Let's do lunch' with the Managing Director gave randomly invited people a direct opportunity to ask questions.*
- Print: *to ensure the integrity of core messages regular news and feature articles were published in the staff magazine. This was also a way of informing staff not directly involved in the programme about the work. Fortnightly newsletters for the Sky speakers and weekly updates for the heads of department also kept them up-to-date throughout the programme.*
- Intranet: *for those with access to the intranet this was a direct way of updating programme news and also served as an archive.*
- e-Mail: *to send both global announcements and attached news to particular audiences, for example, the Sky speakers newsletter. This meant information could be issued regularly without incurring costs.*
- Direct mail: *to kick off the programme a letter from the Managing Director, Tony Ball, was sent to every member of staff.*
- Exhibition: *an exhibition was set up on two different sites, with additional selected panels placed in training centres around the UK. The CRM programme should always maintain a permanent presence in the buildings, especially when a lot of the work was taking place off site.*
- Video: *with around 6500 contact centre staff and 1300 installers, video provided a cost-effective and practical medium to introduce the Managing Director and ensure messages were consistent, regardless of where people worked or their shift pattern.*

Feedback

The return of the 2001 Employee Survey increased 42 per cent on the previous year – outlining improvements achieved.

Evidence of success

A key indicator that messages have been taken on board is shown through the 'Heroes' nominations: a programme that rewards world-beating customer service. People not only understand world-beating customer service but are also demonstrating it through this scheme, sharing their examples with the rest of the business.

Janet Brogan, Communications Director at BskyB, was central to the roll-out of the programme and instrumental in its ongoing success. She devised the 'Lets do lunch' idea, which has changed the way employees interact with senior management. She said:

> When we asked for nominations for people to volunteer to become Sky speakers we had over 400 people respond and the 250 who were successful are now part of a company-wide communications network. We saw a marked change in the types of questions and feedback we were receiving from Sky speakers and at 'Let's do lunch' (with the Managing Director). Early on in the programme these were focused on housekeeping issues; latterly they have shown an understanding of the business direction, vision and culture.
>
> We found that people challenge decisions if they don't feel they adhere to the new culture, demonstrating that they remember the characteristics and values. During culture focus groups people demonstrated an awareness of the values and characteristics and were interested in their implementation.
>
> The behaviour of people along with awareness of values and characteristics has improved. There is evidence of more effective team working, more opportunities for matrix teams enabling us to solve more problems and getting the whole company connected.

References

Campbell, A., Devine, M. and Young, D. (1990). *A Sense of Mission*. Random House Business Books.

Clutterbuck, D. and Kernaghan, S. (1999). *Doing it Different*. Weidenfeld and Nicolson.

Collins, J. C. and Porras, J. I. (2000). *Built to Last*. Random House Business Books.

Goldsmith, W. and Clutterbuck, D. (1998). *The Winning Streak Mark II*. Weidenfeld and Nicolson.

Communication during radical change

This chapter is about the role of communication in the management of change. The truism that the only constant in modern organizations is change is often quoted, but what does it actually mean? In practice organizations institute significant changes for one of two reasons: because the external environment – in terms of technology, societal values and expectations, customer needs or competitive situation – has shifted or can be predicted to shift; and because the internal environment changes (for example, with new leadership).

The vast majority of changes that occur within business organizations are small, largely unnoticed and yet often cumulatively significant. A minor change in recruitment policy, for example, may attract younger, better educated employees, who gradually challenge accepted practices. In a large European bank, for example, the cultural shift this is causing is strongly and visibly supported by top management, to the extent that culture change is occurring without the need for a formal culture change programme.

Other changes, particularly the introduction of new technology, require a greater degree of hands-on management. New technologies are introduced with the aim of increasing efficiency, but in many cases, according to McKinsey consultants Michael Earl and David Feeny (1995), 'what [managers] observe and experience are IS project failures, unrelenting hype about IT, and rising information processing costs'. If managed successfully, however, the study found that technological advances could be the key to a company's success, as in the case of an industry leading retailer which overtook entrenched rivals as a result of the innovative use of IT.

Yet other changes delve deep into the organizational psyche. Usually classed as culture change programmes, these typically result from recognizing that the business vision cannot be sustained with the existing attitudes and behaviours or with the existing relationships between the company and its key stakeholders.

We shall focus in this chapter on the second type of change, although it must be recognized that small, gradual changes need to be identified and managed in the aggregate (Figure 6.1). First, however, let us establish some basics about the nature of organizational change.

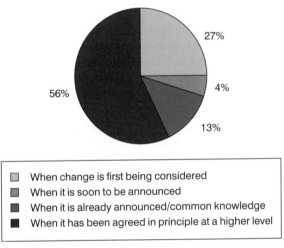

Figure 6.1 When communicators get involved in change

Managing major structural and cultural change emerged in **item**'s most recent survey of internal communication managers (Kernaghan, Clutterbuck and Cage, 2001) as the most substantial areas of involvement for internal communicators, with 70 per cent expecting to support a major change over the following 24 months. However, as Figure 6.1 shows, they are generally only brought into the planning process once all the decisions have been made. Moreover, they concede that communicating change is a responsibility at which they are only moderately successful. Which is rather unfortunate, because it is the activity upon which the function's performance is most likely to be judged by top management!

Various models of change have been developed over the past half-century, but most tend to be somewhat restrictive in what they attempt to describe. Perhaps the most common, in several variations, is a curve that compares the process of adapting to change to that of bereavement. The individual or organization goes through a number of phases, from denial to mourning, acceptance and moving on. The problem with this model is that most changes are not that traumatic. The employee may see the change in positive or neutral terms, perhaps as a great opportunity. The concerns they have may not be with what is lost (indeed, there may be nothing significant to lose) but with the intellectual and emotional effort they will have to make to meet the challenge. To approach all change as if it were a drama, where people need counselling, would be patently ridiculous.

Take the example of two acquisitions, by the same company. One of the acquisitions had been in a shallow decline for several years and the employees had by and large lost confidence in the leadership. Rather than fear being taken over, even though there was a high probability of job losses, the employees welcomed the change of ownership, on the grounds that tough decisions would at last be taken to ensure that as many jobs as possible survived. They also saw wider career opportunities with the new owner. The other acquisition was a long-established manufacturer, where employees held great store by the name and identity of the company. Here, they needed to be helped through the process of understanding why the name had to change and of overcoming their fears about some fairly radical changes in work practice that would make life less comfortable, at least initially. The bereavement model applies in the second case, but is irrelevant in the first, although superficially both were very similar instances.

A more current view of change is that it is *a process of organizational learning*. Figure 6.2 shows how that process typically works at an organizational level. Something in the environment creates a stimulus for change. The leadership can ignore the stimulus, focusing on more pressing issues, or elect to deal with it. A period of reflection results in a set of goals for change, which are then broken down into smaller steps, which allow planning processes to come into play. Implementation is typically a process of trial and error, with activities moderated by feedback from either or both within and outside the organization. The feedback stimulates more reflection, which may in turn moderate the change goals. A similar model applies to teams.

At the individual level, a parallel process occurs. People are made aware of the need to change, but no real progress will be made until they first understand the implications of the change and accept that it applies to them. It is not really surprising that

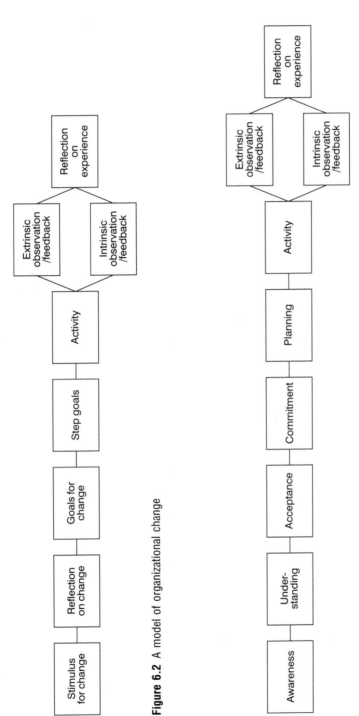

Figure 6.2 A model of organizational change

Figure 6.3 How individuals change

most people, when quizzed about desirable behaviours in the workplace, consistently rate themselves more highly than most of their colleagues. It often takes quite severe feedback around the consequences before people accept that they are poor listeners or bad drivers, for example.

Acceptance, however, is no guarantee of action. That demands commitment, which only comes from a sense of personal contract. The act of verbalizing an intention to change is often essential to the process of commitment, whether the promise is made quietly to oneself, or in front of a group of colleagues. Of course, while genuine commitment to change becomes more powerful when verbalized, there is no such effect for promises which are made as a result of external pressures such as the threat of job losses. In this case the individual may pay lip-service to the new behaviour while rejecting the spirit of the promise.

Even genuine commitment soon fades, unless the individual has a plan of action to begin and to sustain the change through the cycles of experimentation and reflection until the new behaviours have 'stuck' (Figure 6.3). Part of that plan has to include observation and feedback, to bring the individual through the cycle from unconscious incompetence, through conscious incompetence and conscious competence to unconscious competence. (In sport, this is often described as cementing an action into the muscle memory.) As with the organization, it is the combination of extrinsic feedback (what others observe) and intrinsic feedback (what you feel and observe for yourself) that provides the most powerful stimulus for improvement. Feedback also plays another major role: it provides the encouragement and motivation to persevere, even when you encounter significant setbacks. Ideally, once the change has been achieved, the individual is able to reflect back on it and identify lessons that he or she can apply in the next cycle of change.

In both these models, communication is at the heart of the process. However, it is rare to find an organization that has a comprehensive change communication process, which links each phase of change and helps progress from one to the next. More rarely still do companies recognize the phased nature of the interaction between organizational change and individual change, i.e. that some groups of people will move further and faster along the sequence of change than others. Even in the senior management team, it is likely that those within the 'inner cabinet' will have gone through the cycle of awareness to commitment well ahead of those on the outside. The change communication process needs to be structured to take account of these phase differences and to measure where each group is, before taking major steps forward. A case in point is the retailer, which introduced an empowerment programme. Branch managers in the stores chosen to pioneer the process were specially selected and were given time with the business leaders to get used to the ideas. Ordinary employees had briefings and a series of facilitated discussions with their supervisors, and seemed to go along with what was proposed. Stage one of the empowerment programme passed with barely a hitch, as far as the managers could see. But on the cusp of introducing stage two, the employees said they wanted to take the whole discussion back to first principles. What the managers had assumed was commitment, was in reality passive acceptance – 'We'll see how it works out'. This scenario, in one form or another, is enacted time and time again in change programmes.

Why people resist change

Another of the problems with standard models of change is that they do not distinguish between conscious and unconscious resistance, nor between intellectual and emotional resistance. Figure 6.4 shows the four combinations that arise from these distinctions. Conscious intellectual resistance is perhaps the easiest to deal with. Dialogue about the facts, specific intentions and predicted outcomes of the change can be kept at a relatively rational level. Even if there remains some disagreement of interpretation, dissenters will usually come along with the consensus and much good may have been done by surfacing potential problems the change champions had not foreseen. Where people are able to demonstrate that they will be placed at considerable disadvantage by the change, then the door is open to discuss how to accommodate their needs (for example, trading longer travel to work against more opportunities to work from home).

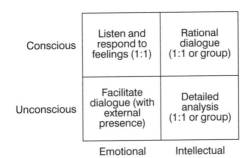

Figure 6.4 Types of change resistance and how best to overcome them

Unconscious intellectual resistance occurs when people perceive that the arguments for change do not hang together, but cannot articulate what precisely is wrong. Although they may express it as 'I've got a bad feeling about this', it is the rational element of their intuition that is active. Dialogue with a strong element of analysis, particularly about assumptions made on both sides, is the key to surfacing these issues, so they can be dealt with on a conscious intellectual level.

Conscious emotional resistance occurs for a variety of reasons, but is often associated with perceived loss of status (e.g. 'you are no longer going to report direct to the head of department'). A different kind of dialogue is needed here. People need to be able to express their feelings, to receive sympathy and to work through the sense of loss. The goal should be to help them move as rapidly as possible to a state of mind where they can either see positive possibilities in the new situation, or at least a way forward that allows them to rebuild their self-esteem. Whereas intellectual resistance may often be dealt with in one or two sessions of dialogue, conscious emotional resistance often takes much more time and more meetings to overcome.

Unconscious emotional resistance is even more demanding on management time, because the individual or group need first to understand why they are being resistant. They may not even be aware that they are blocking the change. It is common for people to believe that their attitudes and behaviours are perfectly all right, when the opposite is true. For example, diversity or equal opportunities training is often an eye-opener for managers who could not previously accept that they were prejudiced or held unacceptable stereotype views.

Another common source of unconscious emotional resistance is guilt – for example, among the survivors after a merger or downsizing. Until people recognize and can deal with these feelings, they will inhibit their ability to perform.

Tackling unconscious emotional resistance demands facilitated dialogue and well-managed feedback that gives people access to aspects of their thinking and feeling they would not normally recognize.

To summarize, conscious intellectual resistance, at one extreme, may be managed in large part through media that educate and inform and can typically be accomplished in the short term. Conscious emotional and unconscious intellectual resistance demand substantially more discussion and the development of understanding, perhaps through briefing groups and may require longer. Unconscious emotional resistance typically requires the establishment of a deeper self-awareness, which generally requires intensive training or one-to-one counselling.

This may take longer still – sometimes months – to remove the internal barriers to change.

Correctly assessing the nature of change resistance and applying the appropriate communication solutions is not easy. The lower people's receptivity to the change message, the more effort will be required to bring about change. *In extremis*, the adage 'if you can't change the people, change the people' may apply. However, a planned approach, which measures all four kinds of resistance and makes available sufficient communication resources to overcome them, is a critical element in effective management of major change.

The worry index

Behind each of these causes of change resistance most of the time are legitimate concerns that arise from uncertainty about the future. Coping with uncertainty can be frightening and stressful, particularly for some personalities and those who have not been regularly exposed to change. (See the brief discussion below on change resilience.) Some of the key questions to acknowledge – even if they cannot always be answered – are contained in an instrument we call the *Worry Index* (included in Chapter 8 on mergers and acquisitions)

The key to managing people's worries and fears seems to be to accept that they are real, to provide information about what *is* known, to reassure people that someone is in charge of the issues outside their control and to help them take steps that increase their own ability either to reduce uncertainty or to open up sufficient options to reduce the level of anxiety they feel.

Co-ordinating change streams

The owners of a change often see it only in a very narrow context. They may, for example, see it as simply a new piece of equipment or amending a set of procedures. But few significant changes happen in isolation. They affect other processes and they almost always require support from the following three change streams:

1 *Infrastructure* describes the physical surroundings, reporting structures, equipment, quality of information sources and so on.
2 *Systems* are the processes, from IT to how people are recruited and promoted, or how financial data is collected and analysed.
3 *People*: the willingness and ability of people to respond appropriately to the change.

Major changes often go wrong because managers either allocate insufficient resources to one or more of the streams, or because they fail to see all three streams as interlinked and mutually supportive. So, information about infrastructure elements of a change may come from the facilities department, systems from IT and about relevant training programmes from HR. The net result? Conflicting data, confusion and a failure to co-ordinate the timing of communication.

Effective change management will integrate the three streams and the communication processes around them.

A structured approach to communicating change

The four pillars of communication (outlined in Chapter 1) provide a robust practical and theoretical framework for communicating change. As with any other communication strategy, it is important to address all four pillars within a coherent approach that uses both direct activity and influence of key partners in the organization.

The starting point for the strategy has to be the business purpose. What precisely needs to change about the culture and why? How will this make a difference to the business and its potential to achieve strategic goals in the medium term and the business vision/mission in the longer term? The internal communication professional cannot and should not provide the answers to these questions; that responsibility lies firmly with the leadership. However, he or she should play a role in helping top management *articulate* the answers (Figure 6.5).

There are three key audiences to be considered in articulating the purpose of the change: the employees, the external stakeholders (normally looked after by the corporate or external communication function) and the leadership group itself. In general, top teams do not invite either the internal or corporate communication function to help in ensuring that they have a clear and consistent perception of the change purpose within their own team. If they use anyone at all, it tends to be an externally resourced strategy consultant who facilitates appropriate discussions. Such external help, however, tends to be short term. Where the message often goes awry most seriously is when the changes are being rolled out and have to be explained and re-explained in the light of the realities of implementation. There is an internal facilitation role to be played that involves challenging the leaders about what they mean and why, how committed they are, what they really expect of the organization and its people, and how unified they are in the meaning they ascribe to the

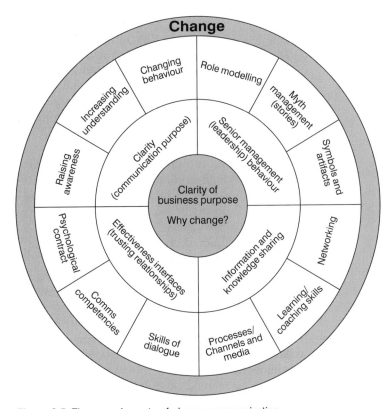

Figure 6.5 The core elements of change communication

words. This is not an easy role. It demands the skill and courage to 'speak truth to power' and to be an effective bearer of bad news, in placing the spotlight upon any disunity of vision among the leaders.

Communication purpose

Out of the business purpose of the change come the four key elements of the change communication plan. *Communication purpose* translates the business case for change into specific activities, based on the degree of change which the organization hopes to bring about in its people. There are three basic levels of personal change:

- Raise awareness.
- Build understanding.
- Change behaviour.

Different audiences in the organization will require different degrees of clarity. For example, a restructure of the IT function, to make it more sensitive and responsive to the needs of internal customers, may require substantial behaviour changes among IT staff, significant understanding of what it all means by the managers of customer departments, who will have to adapt some processes and accept different outputs from IT, and a broad awareness by employees in general, who will not be so directly affected by the changes.

The communication process appropriate for each of these levels of change is likely to vary considerably, too. At the awareness level, there is likely to be an emphasis on informing, which will normally occur through predominantly one-way media, such as memos, articles in the employee newspaper, videos or traditional cascade briefings. To build understanding, a greater level of discussion is needed, in which people can ask questions, raise concerns and give feedback. The more the discussion moves towards consulting and involving, the greater the level of understanding will be, and the more likely people will be to accept and work with the changes. To change behaviour, however, requires dialogue and, if possible, some measure of participation in how the changes will be implemented.

Trusting interfaces

The quality of the trust between individuals and departments (and between both of these and the leadership) will also have a major impact on the organization's ability to make change happen. Unfortunately, trust is not something you can switch on, on demand. It typically requires a lot of purposeful effort over a considerable period. A large European manufacturing company provides a good example of some of the problems. It had grown primarily through acquisition from a base in France, absorbing businesses across Europe, each of which had very different cultures from its own. Despite all attempts at integration (perhaps in some cases because of them), the level of trust between the centre and the local leadership remained low and this was reflected in the attitudes and behaviours of people at all levels. When top management decided it simply had to create one culture, taking the best elements from the diversity within the group, it met a great deal of quiet but immovable resistance. Without the groundwork to create trusting relationships to begin with, a far greater effort would have been required to achieve cultural integration than the leaders were prepared to put in. The problems continue.

We shall explore the international culture issues in more detail later in this chapter, but for now let us concentrate on the practical steps an organization can take to build trusting relationships. Trust levels can be much lower than top management believes. A study for the UK Trades Union Congress by the London School of Economics (TUC/LSE, 2001) reported that only 38 per cent of employees trust their employers. Against such an attitudinal barrier, it is hardly surprising that covert resistance undermines otherwise well-crafted strategies.

The first element to tackle in building trust between employees and the organization is the psychological contract. One of the biggest keys to successful change is to understand and manage the impact it has on the expectations the employees have of the organization and vice versa. (See Chapter 4 on stakeholder communications for more about the psychological contract.)

Another important way of establishing trust where it has not been strong before is to build openness into relationships. A very high proportion of poor relationships occur because people do not understand the values, perceptions or circumstances of others. The less we are able to 'connect', the less we ascribe positive intent to what they do and say. This problem is often particularly acute across national or ethnic cultures, but occurs in many other situations, too. For example, an employee who was avoided by others, because she was seen as a little strange and erratic in her behaviour, was readily accepted when it was revealed that her occasional oddity was the result of a serious brain injury sustained in a car accident. Once they understood the behaviour, colleagues were able to recognize and accommodate it.

Although many companies have openness as one of their corporate values, few are adept at translating it into practical processes and instinctive behaviour. Genuine openness involves:

- honesty – both intellectual and emotional – in explaining situations and issues to employees
- ensuring that information is freely available to employees on a 'want to know' rather than 'need to know' basis
- encouraging people to cross hierarchical boundaries to find things out or offer information
- demonstrating effective listening behaviours – showing a genuine interest and desire for different ideas and opinions
- encouraging and giving constructive criticism
- admitting mistakes and the lessons learned from them
- developing relationships with individuals and making it possible for them to discuss personal issues which may affect their work.

Open behaviour benefits the business in many ways. For a change process it overcomes hidden fears such as: 'Are there things they are not telling me?' 'Will there really be only a small number of redundancies?' It allows people's concerns and suggestions to emerge readily, so that they can be tackled in support of the changes. It reduces the build-up of hidden resistance and ensures that the feedback top management receives is more genuine and accurate.

This latter point is worthy of further explanation. Some years ago, we were asked by a subsidiary of Unilever to help develop a more effective change management process. To provide a practical starting point for what actually happened in the organization, we tracked what had happened in three major changes, which had been introduced over the previous eighteen months, by asking people at each level of the organization to tell their story of what occurred. Top management's perception of the changes were somewhat more positive than those of middle managers, and much rosier than those of shop-floor supervisors and operators. The people at the sharp end pointed out that they never had time to embed one change before the next washed over them. What looked from above like a smooth adaptation was in fact a series of quick fixes. Their complaints had generally been dismissed as whinging, and middle managers, not wanting to appear inadequate, had consistently fed top management a more positive picture of implementation than was warranted. And, of course, top management had responded by introducing yet more change, in the belief that all was reasonably well.

More open behaviours would have encouraged genuine dialogue around the practicalities of introducing change. They would also have enabled the changes to be seen not as wave after wave of interruptions to people's work, but as steps towards a bigger shared goal. So why is not open behaviour the norm in most organizations? Part of the answer is that some people (including leaders) just do not hold this value; some managers are afraid of losing prestige, control or some other element of traditional management style. But another common reason is that some managers lack either or both the competence and the structures to be truly open.

Communication competence (dealt with in detail in Chapter 9) is essential if people are to have the confidence that they can explain what they mean, what they feel and what they observe – in other words, if they are to be genuinely open in their relationships with others. Few managers will admit to having problems communicating, yet the reality is that very few have the full portfolio of skills required to be open communicators. Many may be excellent presenters, but poor listeners. The abilities to explain ideas clearly and help others to express themselves more clearly are also less common than they might be. The internal communication function should play an active role in establishing both the skills levels in communication and the impact of these on employee behaviour. It should also partner with HR in providing practical help in improving communication competence through appropriate training.

Much the same applies to the promotion of dialogue. In recent research (conducted on behalf of Hertfordshire Training and Enterprise Council in 1998) into the effectiveness of various types of team, we observed that teams that learned well together (and were therefore more adaptable and positive towards change) created frequent opportunities for dialogue, both one to one and as a whole team. Having dialogue, of course, is not the same as having team meetings. It goes far beyond discussion, giving people the opportunity to explore issues in real depth and with genuine willingness to both listen to and learn from the views of others.

When we discussed dialogue previously, in the context of the communication purpose, we were concerned with the stimulation of interchange to the leadership's agenda. In the context of building trust, we are concerned much more with the multitude of interchanges that occur from day to day to the agendas of the employees and their teams. Because trust is generally a two-way emotion (it is difficult to trust someone who does not trust you!), it is built up gradually, through many interactions.

Trust-building is not normally seen as a skill or competence, yet it does take skill to build trust, especially with people who we do not immediately take to. Within the team, in particular, it is (or should be) the manager's responsibility to help people build trusting relationships. Again there is a role for the internal communication function, working with HR, to:

- help people develop trust building skills of dialogue
- provide expert facilitation in helping team members, or different teams, to engage in trust-building dialogue
- provide the infrastructure to support dialogue and open behaviours.

The latter is more difficult than it sounds, because many of the decisions that establish the communication environment are in the hands of other functions. Genuine dialogue typically requires a quiet meeting place, away from interruptions. Yet these are becoming scarcer and scarcer in many companies. It also requires not just permission from line managers for people to take time out to talk about issues that may not seem urgent, but their active encouragement.

One of the most damaging myths of current working practice is that people are more efficient if their work is paced to ensure they are always busy. In reality, people are most efficient and effective when they are able to vary routines between concentrated task activities, play and opportunities to reflect. Reflective space and reflective dialogue are essential for both individuals and teams. Reflective space is an opportunity for discovery through dialogue. For an individual this involves asking questions of oneself to achieve the level of understanding of an issue, often from different perspectives, that opens the door to insights. From such insights come new tactics, greater self-awareness and greater ability to manage oneself and others, and the establishment of clearer priorities. People sometimes describe personal reflective space (PRS) as 'giving myself a good talking to' or inviting an imaginary second person into their head.

Relationships like coaching and mentoring solidify this extra presence: the other person helps you work through issues by asking questions that lead to insight, but they are likely to ask more of you, from a wider range of different perspectives, and to be less likely to let you off the hook if a line of exploration becomes too uncomfortable. The same process can and does work at team level. But teams need to learn the skills of managing dialogue before they can apply it effectively, otherwise, they sink back into the behaviours of discussion and debate (or worse, conflict) that characterize most team meetings.

The internal communication function can help by providing, with HR, appropriate training in the skills of dialogue. It can also promote the cause of reflective space, and seek champions for the concept at top management level. It can insist on having a voice in accommodation design. In the handful of cases where communication professionals have taken this role seriously, they have, for example, been able to persuade the facilities department to attach meeting size informal spaces to coffee areas, to accept a higher ratio of meeting space to headcount and to allow spare space in the communication function offices specifically for the purpose of extra meeting rooms.

An obvious way around the meeting space problem is to conduct online dialogues. There are numerous problems with this approach, not least the difficulty of ensuring that everyone is in an environment, where they will not be interrupted and the difficulty of maintaining any sort of discipline on an exchange where several people may be making separate points at the same time. However, creating themed chat-room dialogues about issues of mutual concern to leaders and employees is a useful additional approach.

Knowledge sharing

As the example of the Unilever subsidiary above demonstrates, the effectiveness of change management is easily undermined by failure to gather and share information about the progress of change. However, knowledge sharing involves a number of other essential activities, including the dissemination of good practice, tapping into the vast store of tacit knowledge held by experienced employees and managers, and ensuring that people know where and how to access information that will help them be more effective.

The three tactical areas, where internal communication can influence these activities are processes (channels and media), learning and coaching practice, and networking. In a major change programme, the probability is that the organization will need to use all existing media, along with new ones, to ensure that people have the maximum opportunity to generate and access a wide range of information, directly or indirectly related to the change. These information needs can be divided into three levels:

- macro – related to understanding of the big picture and how the changes are progressing across the organization as a whole
- mini – related to team goals and priorities within the framework of the change programme
- micro – what the individual needs to know to implement the changes in their own work and relationships with others.

At each level, the health of information sharing can be gleaned from the extent to which information is exchanged freely in all directions – up, down and across the organization – without regard for departmental or hierarchical boundaries. Information transparency is the goal.

Transparency implies quality rather than quantity; ease of draw down rather than ease of pour down. These characteristics of information exchange do not happen automatically, they require continued support, especially from the centre, and continuous adaptation of systems to adapt to changes in people and their needs to know, to be consulted and to be able to share what they have learned.

However, support from the centre does not mean control. Information transparency occurs most easily when people are encouraged and enabled, rather than told, to use media. For example, one of the classic conundrums of western businesses is the failure or, at best, mediocre performance of suggestion schemes, especially when compared with Japanese organizations. Figures vary and there are some differences in what is measured, but some Japanese companies appear to receive at least twenty-five times more suggestions for improvements each year than do their western counterparts, even after many years of quality programmes. The primary differences are not cultural, as is so often claimed, but in the communication infrastructure.

The idea of relying on a suggestion box would be laughed at in the Japanese company. It is not immediate, it requires a significant effort on the part of the employee, there is no real-time recognition, and there is little opportunity to test and hone an idea with colleagues before presenting it. In the Japanese teams, ideas are collected by employees specifically tasked with recording them *at the point of impact*. If a worker has a problem at a machine, he can discuss it with the colleague as he works. Either they develop a solution together and/or they share their ideas with other colleagues in team meetings. Western companies that enthusiastically adopted quality circles generally missed the point. By the time the circle meets, only the major, constantly recurring and most obvious problems are remembered and discussed.

Some of the questions that need to be asked in assessing how well the available media contribute to change are:

- To what extent are people aware that they exist, and how to access them?
- Are they primarily one-way, two-way or multidirectional (i.e. anyone can access and contribute to them)?
- Does each channel have an 'owner' and a process for consulting with other departments about its quality and relevance?
- Does each medium have clear communication objectives?
- How valuable and reliable does the medium appear to its audience?

When a change programme is initiated, the internal communication function can assist by monitoring message consistency across the various channels and media. Is one channel proving parsimonious with detail, while another discusses issues much more freely? The function can also advise on what media are most appropriate for each communication purpose and, where appropriate, manage those media on behalf of the change programme.

Coaching and mentoring are very powerful methods of sharing. In general, coaches tend to help people develop knowledge and skills related to their current tasks or to specific behavioural changes; mentors take a broader perspective, look-ing at the development of the whole individual over a longer time period and focusing less on current performance than the development of wisdom and wider understanding. Both are essential elements in managing change.

Mentors often play a highly valuable role in helping others cope with the stress of change. When reporting structures and responsibilities are changing, teams being dispersed and support networks disrupted, a mentor can provide an island of stability, in which the employee can seek refuge. Mentors help put changes into perspective, stimulate mentees to plan how to get the best out of change and challenge the mentee's attitudes and assumptions, so that they examine critically how they are responding to change.

Whether the company opts for a formal or informal approach to coaching and/or mentoring (and there are good arguments for and against each, according to circumstance and purpose), to make this kind of activity intrinsic and a part of the culture requires communication support. Training is the most obvious and basic form of support, but participants also find it useful to have a database of available mentors, information about how to be an effective coach, mentor or learner and opportunities to bring mentors together as part of a continuous development network. While the ownership of the coaching or mentoring programme is likely to rest with HR, the effective use of communication resources is a factor in almost all programmes that become self-sustaining. Where a network of mentors already exists, making them aware of planned changes and their implications helps initiate constructive debate about what is planned and provides a valuable temperature check on the organization.

One of the most positive aspects of the information revolution is that it has become far, far easier to establish networks. Because change tends to disrupt existing networks, the capacity to build new networks, both within and outside the organization, is an emerging core competence. Part of this competence rests with the individuals, who may need training in how to establish informa-tional and influential relationships quickly. But the organization itself can also develop the capacity to stimulate new networks whenever they can help the process of change. BT, for example, has been highly successful in developing diversity networks, in support of radical change in its equal opportunities policies. (The change was less in the policy than in the commitment to putting it into practice.) Other organizations have stimulated networks to share knowledge in various disciplines, from exotic materials to compensation policy, parenting to work–life balance. There is an expanding role here for the internal communication function to support change by:

- recognizing communities of interest and encouraging them to share knowledge, experience and concerns
- ensuring that the technology available eases the creation and maintenance of these networks
- training volunteers in how to manage a community of interest (which may be permanent or temporary, for the period of change implementation).

Leadership behaviour

The CEO of a large European chemicals company instigated and attempted to force through a major culture change. There was one fatal flaw in his strategy: his own behaviour was entirely counter to what he was demanding from everyone else. Something had to give. It did. He lost his job in less than eighteen months.

Whenever major change is required, employees look to top management to provide leadership in a number of ways. They expect the leaders to identify closely with the changes, to devote a considerable amount of time to explaining the purpose and implications of the changes, to exhibit a passion for achieving the change goals and to be role models for any adjustments in behaviour that are required.

Being an active role model is not easy. It is not just about walking the talk – though that is difficult enough. It is also about developing a high level of awareness and sensitivity to what others conclude from what we say and do. Such awareness comes partly from personal observation, but it also comes from objective (and sometimes subjective) feedback. Perhaps the first question any CEO should ask when initiating a change that demands different behaviours of other people is, 'What do I have to change in my behaviour?' And the second is, 'How will I know how successful I am being?'

The leaders will almost certainly need some help and support in articulating these personal change objectives and gathering feedback on how effective a role model each is proving to be. If people perceive that they are poor role models, it is almost inevitable that there will be either apathy or resistance to the changes, even though employees may at a rational level accept that they make sense.

Because so few employees have regular contact with the leaders of a large business, role modelling tends to take place at a distance and to be closely bound up with executive credibility.

A key tool in building both is 'myth management' (a term that requires some care in pronunciation, if people are to understand it correctly). Myth management relates to the stories which people tell about organizations and key people within them. Charismatic business leaders generate a host of stories, which often become amplified as they are repeated, resulting from surprising things they do or say. More than anything else, such stories shape the informal culture, defining what is expected and not expected, approved and disapproved.

Really effective leaders instinctively know when to make a dramatic statement or gesture. And times of major change are often when such gestures have maximum impact. A classic story in this regard concerns a company that had to make substantial cutbacks, which would demand sacrifices from many people. The week the changes were announced, a vehicle transporter appeared in the car park. All the top team drove their executive cars up the ramps and collected much cheaper models.

So yet another key question to ask when major change is considered is, 'How shall we ensure that the kind of stories people tell support the change objectives?' It is remarkable how readily opportunities arise to recognize people publicly and spontaneously for putting new behaviours into practice. Opportunities for dramatic gestures may be more difficult to find, but it is almost always possible. Some further examples:

- When introducing 360-degree appraisal, the leaders of a company insisted on being the first to undergo the process and on sharing the results with employees in general.
- One managing director regularly took his turn on reception to set the standard for customer care within the organization.
- Human Resources employees and management staff at Mount Rushmore, one of America's best known national parks, take an active hand, leading by example to show new hires what they want. This may include flipping hamburgers, bagging merchandise, stocking shelves, vacuuming floors. Their HR director explained, 'it's a team effort to get the job done and to make the experience of the visiting guest a memorable one'.

A third factor, which can be managed, is what Harvard academic, Ed Schein, calls symbols and artefacts. These are the physical manifestations of the culture – the buildings, the way people dress, whether there are separate dining rooms and car parking spaces for executives, and so on. The question here is, 'Are there physical changes we can make that will reinforce the change message?' For example, moving to an open-plan office format reinforces the move to a less hierarchical culture. One company was able to resolve many issues around the handling of customer orders by co-locating the manufacturing and marketing departments (marketing had previously been located in the head office).

Integrating the elements of change communication

Addressing all these issues within a coherent communication plan will help the organization implement change with the support of employees and with a common sense of purpose. It cannot compensate for poor technical planning, inadequate software or insufficient resourcing. But it can help to expose problems earlier and ensure they are discussed openly and without defensiveness.

Although it is a communication plan, its primary ownership should rest with top management and the various partners, such as HR and marketing. As we shall see in the chapter on communication competence, the communication professional needs to develop a high level of skills in influencing and alliance building at top management level. This in turn demands the strategic awareness to understand and reflect the full significance of change, on behalf of the leadership, and the strategic listening skills to reflect to the leadership the extent to which the message has been accepted and translated into action by the employees.

Case study

Communicating change at GKN

When C. K. Chow was appointed chief executive of global industrial company GKN, he recognized that tough competition, industry consolidation and globalization were changing their marketplace. GKN's conservative engineering culture, focused on quality and customer care, was too slow-moving for the company's new operating environment. The company needed to preserve its reputation for quality while losing the perfectionism which held it back from speed and innovation.

The company began its change programme by developing workshops for the top 500 managers to consider the changes that were required and how they would be made to happen in the individual businesses. The outcome was local action plans which senior managers took back to their teams.

Although the programme was generally considered a success, the change was not filtering through the organization as fast as senior management had hoped. One manager described how her own perceptions altered as a result of the programme. Her initial reaction was, 'So what? It's just another lot of statements. We have had these things routinely through our history'. She later said, 'As I was given the opportunity to work with it through the workshops my opinion changed. There was consistency in what we were saying and it was all quite inspiring. The problem was that not everyone had the opportunity to discover this for themselves'.

In an attempt to remedy this, GKN appointed a dedicated internal communication professional and created a communication campaign to all employees aimed at:

- *telling a consistent, positive story*
- *communicating what was working about the change*
- *making everyone feel like part of the new GKN culture.*

The campaign, entitled 'You make the difference', was built around a strong brand, treating employees as customers and 'selling' them the message of change (for further details of this approach, see Chapter 7 on brand).

Alongside the communication campaign, numerous changes took place, including an increase in managers crossing 'borders' to work in other areas of the business and gain more understanding of their place in the organization as a whole. To support the new, more inclusive culture, the intranet was made available to everyone via a mixture of personal computers and intranet kiosks, the number of languages used in global communication was increased and a mentoring programme was introduced.

After these and other initiatives were introduced, qualitative research was carried out which validated the overall success of the change programme.

Branding change

A useful way of looking at change in a large organization is the change funnel. The typical situation is that there are dozens, perhaps hundreds, of significant changes planned a year or more out. Each function has its own strategic and tactical goals and feels obliged to put forward plans for increasing efficiency, keeping up with competitors' technology, improving customer service and so on. At this point, the widest part of the funnel, the changes are generally discrete – they may fit within a very broad corporate strategy, but they are at best only loosely linked to each other (Figure 6.6).

At the narrow end of the funnel is the reality of change capacity – how much change people in the organization can manage over a six-month period. Few companies attempt to measure this in any meaningful way, but it is a critical part of effective change

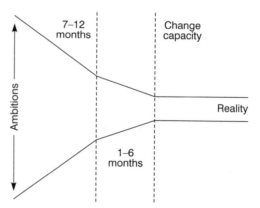

Figure 6.6 The change funnel

management. Try to push too much change through and people become overloaded and overstressed; their day-to-day work suffers and too many corners are cut in the changes that are implemented. People feel obliged to report successes where there are in reality only partial achievements. Top management (who may often regard a problem as solved once it has left their desks) becomes frustrated and may respond by trying to push yet more change through. Push too little change through and the organization may struggle to meet its strategic goals.

There are two obvious solutions to this bottleneck. One is to enlarge the size of the narrow end of the funnel – to increase people's capacity to absorb change. Daryl R. Conner's (1992) work on change resilience is highly useful here. He argues that people have an in-built level of change resilience, partly related to experience and partly to personality. The degree to which a change is accepted is related not just to the amount of disruption the change causes, but to the extent to which it disrupts expectations (the psychological contract – see above). Therefore people can be supported in absorbing change not only by communicating the change itself, but also by taking the time to work through its implications with those affected and to achieve their commitment to the idea of change.

The other method of expanding the capacity of the funnel is to follow the same principles as modern telecommunication technology – to chunk up change, like data, into larger 'packets' which can be sent through the bottleneck in a continuous stream. The key to doing so lies, first, in how the changes are aggregated into larger elements and, second, in how these are identified or 'branded'.

People will generally accept a lot of small changes, if they can see that they are all part of a larger initiative. It becomes easier for them to see why each change is needed and what the cumulative effect will be. Unfortunately, many companies parcel out changes in chunks too small to see the whole picture. It is rather like giving ten people different bits of a washing machine to assemble, without a plan of the whole. The chances of errors and misfits are greatly increased and the level of enthusiasm for the task much lower.

The six months before changes are launched is the time to pull them together into a small number of clearly themed initiatives. Each requires a straightforward rationale and statement of impact (both internal and external), a champion among the leadership team and a communication plan. At the launch, the big picture is explained, and significant effort needs to be exerted to ensure people understand and accept the need for change. The project plan, with all the expected sub-initiatives explained in brief, is an essential part of this stage and it is important that every team likely to be affected has a chance to discuss its implications and feed back concerns or additional ideas. Subsequently, as each sub-initiative is launched, it is linked strongly to the umbrella theme.

Branding the change – giving it an identity, with an emotive name and supporting design – reinforces this process. Granada's Charles Allen argues that 'People don't like change, so they love the idea of it having a beginning and an ending'. He always brands change programmes, because 'people associate the negatives of restructuring with that brand, and once you've made the reorganization, you can shut the brand down. Constant restructuring is like dragging a plant up by the roots all the time to see if it is growing'.

Branding change also allows people to question the detail of sub-initiatives, to check whether a planned change really does support the principles and values behind the larger goal. Jack Welch, former CEO of GE, endorses this view: 'Companies need overarching themes to create change. If it's just somebody pushing a gimmick or a program, without an overarching theme, you can't get through the wall.'

Case study

Communicating change at Coors Brewers

The prolonged sale of Bass Brewers resulted in a long period of uncertainty, but effective communication meant employees and the business did not suffer.

Employees at Bass Brewers, now Coors, faced a long period of uncertainty during the two years from former parent Bass plc putting the business up for sale in January 2000, to the eventual completion of a purchase by US brewer Coors in February 2002.

In the summer of 2000 it looked like the waiting might be over, when Interbrew bought the business from Bass plc. The DTI blocked the acquisition, however, and months of legal wrangling followed as lawyers and politicians decided the fate of the business.

A decision was eventually reached and Bass Brewers was divided up, with Interbrew retaining the Scottish and Irish operations and the England and Wales business being sold to Coors. Coors Brewers Limited was born in February 2002 – after twenty-five months of uncertainty.

One thing the communication team realized early on in the ownership saga was that the rules, the agendas and the timescales were completely out of the hands of the business and its employees. In most organizations this would have had an adverse affect on employee morale and, ultimately, on commercial performance.

Lesley Allman, Head of Communications, Coors Brewers, says:

We weren't in control of the sale process, so all we could do was keep people up to speed with the principles, the milestones, etc. We couldn't answer any specific questions on the future of our business, its brands or its people. Instead, we concentrated on what our people could control – business as usual – brewing and marketing great beers.

Lesley adds: 'Looking back, 2001 was the company's best ever year in terms of performance throughout its 225 year history. We smashed all targets, employees got their bonuses and our staff retention figure was 6 per cent – the same as usual for us and significantly lower than the national average.'

This was due to employees' dedication to 'business as usual'. The company already had strong brands in the form of Carling, Worthington, Reef, Grolsch, Caffreys and Hooch. It just had to continue building on these and keep satisfying its customers.

Maintaining morale and motivation was the communications teams' number one priority and it achieved this in a number of effective ways.

Ownership

All employees were in the same boat; none of them knew how long the process would take or what the outcome would be. It was important to be open with staff to avoid rumours.

The DTI and other parties made announcements with little or no warning. In these situations, speed is vital if the company is to maintain credibility and avoid employees hearing things first from the media.

This is where a well-established intranet, accessible to virtually all employees played a crucial role. Within minutes of announcements being made, they were made available to employees, often with company commentary accompanying them.

Intranet announcements were supplemented with a series of face-to-face and cascade briefings that were used to give employees the opportunity to ask questions and comment upon important announcements shortly after they were made. Occasionally, publications and CEO letters to employees' homes were used to reinforce important information, provide analysis and ensure key messages were understood.

'As well as informing our employees about the ownership process, we really wanted to involve them', says Lesley Allman. 'Feedback had shown that they really wanted the deal (with Interbrew) to go ahead, so we encouraged them to write to their local MP calling for their support.'

The result was hundreds of employee letters, which were not only good for morale, but provided valuable local public relations opportunities wherever the company employed significant numbers of people.

'We helped people as much as possible with contact names and addresses, but we stopped short of actually writing the letters for them,' says Lesley. 'As a result, the letters weren't just quick scribbles, they were people's real feelings, written with their hearts and minds.'

Although the Interbrew deal was ultimately blocked by the DTI, keeping employees involved and informed throughout the process had built a level of trust that helped see the company through the further uncertain times that still lay ahead.

Business as usual

In addition to 'ownership' communication, a steady flow of 'business as usual' communication was maintained throughout. All the company's communication channels were utilized to demonstrate the importance of maintaining focus and the positive results of doing so. Such communications tended to reinforce at least one of the three themes that employees had been introduced to and had embraced during this time. They were: inspire our people, smash our targets and crush our competition.

'These were simple messages that our employees could relate to,' explains Lesley. 'They also understood that if all three were achieved, company performance would be good and everyone would be rewarded with bonus payments. That certainly focused people's minds.'

Tracking employee opinion

In order to keep track of employee opinion during this period, simple e-mail surveys were issued at regular intervals. The same five questions *were asked each time. These related to feeling about the acquisition and about the company's communications. Results were encouraging. In a typical survey, 92 per cent of respondents said they understood the ownership situation and 78 per cent were positive about the acquisition, up 11 per cent from the previous survey.*

In terms of communication, 75 per cent believed that they had received just the right amount of information from the company and a further 77 per cent felt that they had enough opportunity to ask questions about the acquisition.

Not only did Bass's communication strategy help to motivate employees during a difficult and uncertain period in the company's history, maintaining their morale and building trust, it also affected its business targets, resulting in its best year ever in 2001.

Changing the culture

Less than a couple of decades ago, most companies would have expected to expend considerable effort maintaining their cultures. A stable culture, it was believed, was a hallmark of success, because everyone associated with the organization knew where they stood and what the company wanted of them. Best selling books such as *In Search of Excellence* (Peters and Waterman, 1982) reinforced that view. Companies that did not abandon that view fairly quickly are mostly not around any more. They have been absorbed, if they were lucky, into companies that recognize the competitive reality of operating in rapidly changing environments. Cultures that give competitive advantage today may not do so tomorrow – in a study of companies that have succeeded by being radically different in culture (Clutterbuck and Kernaghan, 1999), we found that it does not take many decades for the differences to be absorbed into the background of business and society. (Few people would think of Levi Strauss as a maverick company, but it was radically different in culture, especially with regard to how it treats employees. Levi Strauss has not abandoned its culture. Other companies have simply caught up, to the extent that its values have become pretty much the norm among good employers.)

Indeed, today's culture may be a liability tomorrow. The vast majority of radical change in corporations seems to arise from the top recognizing that it is impossible to create positive differentiation – or even to run with the pack – without major changes to the ways people think, behave and make decisions.

But what exactly do we mean by culture?

One of the most respected authorities on the nature and implications of culture is Professor Ed Schein, of the Sloan School of Management at MIT. In his analysis, culture is a process of social learning and is composed of three main components:

1 Basic assumptions – how the organization or society relates to its environment; how it perceives the nature of reality, time and space, human nature and the appropriateness of relationships. Basic assumptions are often taken for granted and are rarely expressed consciously.
2 Values – what people hold to be important. For example, people from a Latin American background are likely to place more importance on family obligations than work obligations; North Americans are traditionally the opposite.
3 Artefacts and creations – technology, art, visible and audible behaviour patterns. These are typically 'visible but not decipherable'.

In Schein's analysis these three factors are continuously interacting. Recognizing and/or acknowledging them provides a window on five key areas, where consensus is necessary within the organization: on the core mission or primary task, on the specific goals and timescales to achieve them, on the means to achieve the goals, on how progress towards them is measured and on remedial and repair strategies.

The role of communication in helping to bring about culture change, then, is to:

- create the kind of dialogue that brings basic assumptions, values and artefacts into the open
- enable people to question whether these assumptions, values and artefacts – and the consensus built around them – are still helpful and relevant
- relate behaviour change back to the assumptions, values and artefacts, so that people are aware of the deeper changes they may have to make
- measure how these indicators of culture are changing (for example, to what extent have people's values about customers shifted towards being more empathetic?).

None of this happens quickly. Conversions on the road to Damascus are rare and intensely individual. It takes a great deal of time and pain to change any of these indicators of culture. It also takes a large measure of *positive intent*, by which we mean that people see the point of change, accept the fairness of it (a major barrier in equal opportunities), accept that it will bring specific benefits, and the ratio of effort to reward is sufficiently positive. The greater the shift required in beliefs and assumptions, the more effort will be required. Communication at all levels and through a wide variety of media will be needed to create positive intent, which is just the baseline. Supporting people through the change process, as described earlier in this chapter, and celebrating its achievement will also demand a lot of effort.

The experiences of a major UK electronics company illustrate these issues well.

Culture change and structural change

One of the revelations for a much earlier generation of managers came from the management pioneer, Igor Ansoff (1965), who pointed out what now seems obvious to us, that *structure follows strategy*. Successful businesses do not craft a strategy to fit the way the business is structured; they adjust their structures to fit the demands of their strategy. Many legal partnerships in the UK- and US-dominated international accounting partnerships have learned this lesson in recent decades. In order to compete for financial resources, they have had to abandon the strict partnership model and establish very different structures.

When ICL's strategy called for it to make the transition from a product company to a service company (from computer manufacturer to IT service provider), its CEO, Keith Todd, knew that it was essential to engage its people in the culture change. Six months' worth of work with the top 500 managers failed to deliver the extent or rapidity of transition the company required, so Todd set to work to engage all 22 000 employees in contributing to the change. A cross-functional change team set to work to create a process which would reach everyone and help them recognize the contribution that they, as individuals, could make.

The team settled on a process of dialogue based around 'WorkMats' depicting the company's history, future, vision, strategy and goals. Groups of three or four people discussed the ideas and captured their thoughts in specially designed learning guides. The groups were selected to bring together diverse parts of the business, and were led by volunteer facilitators. The process was heavily publicized, and involvement and feedback took off after responses to the first sessions were published on the company intranet. Interestingly, although there was some cynicism about the programme, the process tended to elicit more support and enthusiasm for the company's strategy and the changes that were taking place.

Summary

Change is more than a constant. It is the ultimate opportunity; and the ultimate threat. Building a change-resilient company, which is able to respond swiftly and in an agile manner to change opportunities, demands instinctive communication processes that permeate the fabric of the organization. These take time to build and need constant maintenance, as they, too, need to be able to change rapidly to adjust to new needs and new structures.

The starting point, in our view, is for leaders to see change and communication as an inseparable couple. Whenever change is planned, communication must be planned. The planning processes are not sequential, however, but in parallel, for effective communication can shape and structure the planning of change in ways that will make implementation more targeted, faster and more sustainable.

References

Ansoff, I. (1965). *Corporate Strategy*. McGraw-Hill.

Clutterbuck, D. and Kernaghan, S. (1999). *Doing it Different*. Weidenfeld and Nicolson.

Conner, D. R. (1992). *Managing at the Speed of Change*. Wiley.

Earl, M. J. and Feeny, D. F. (1995). Is your CIO adding value? *McKinsey Quarterly*, 2, 144–161.

Kernaghan, S., Clutterbuck, D. and Cage, S. (2001). *Transforming Internal Communication*. Business Intelligence.

Peters, T. J. and Waterman, R. H. (1982). *In Search of Excellence*. Harper and Row.

Trades Union Congress/London School of Economics (TUC/LSE) (2001). *Workplace Employee Relations Survey*. TUC/LSE.

Communicating the brand: the pivotal role of employees

The concept of brand has permeated corporate thinking deeply in the past decade. From a concept largely confined to marketing, brand management has become a core organizational competence. But precisely what people mean by brand differs considerably. For some, brand is an expression of the corporate personality – how the organization is viewed by various audiences. For others, it is a set of emotional and eidetic labels aimed at stimulating specific behaviours in targeted customers. It may also be a tool to focus employee attention on a specific programme of change, or a set of design templates. Each or any combination of these may be accurate, according to the circumstances. But the plethora of meanings makes communicating the brand a complex responsibility.

To sort out this confusion, it helps first to distinguish between personality and identity. Corporate identity has to do with external perceptions. Corporate identity specialists aim to provide clarity and consistency around simple and memorable statements (both verbal and visual) that will shape how external audiences perceive the organization vis-à-vis other organizations. These audiences are primarily customers, but intermediaries, investors and the broader community may also be targets of corporate identity programmes.

Corporate personality is basically an expression of the dominant culture (there may be many cultures within an organization). It reflects what the organization believes about itself, how it behaves and the degree of consistency between these. While corporate identity is informed by both vision and values (with a bias towards the former) a corporate personality must be grounded in the organization's values.

The concept of brand management encompasses both identity and personality. It implies some form of manipulation of perceptions, along with adaptations of behaviour, to ensure that the image and the reality are reasonably consistent. Attempts to change identity in ways that conflict with personality almost always fail. A classic example is 'The listening bank' where no one listened.

Managers often assume that the brand is how *they want* people to perceive the company. In reality, brand is how people *do* see the company. Brand management can also be seen as the process of aligning as closely as possible the company's ambitions for how it wants to be perceived with the real world of how people do see it. Brand communication is a process for persuading people to adapt their perceptions accordingly. Critical factors in achieving this include:

- the existing level of consistency between how the company wants to be seen and what it actually does
- the accumulated experiences of each audience in dealing with the company
- the extent, to which people are influenced by peer opinions
- the category of organization, to which people assign this company, and how they feel about this category in general
- the extent, to which the organization is able to establish its own uniqueness of identity.

Brand values are the principles or concepts that underpin the brand. They must reflect the corporate personality as well as the essential elements of the customer promise. The simpler these are, the better. The success of the no-frills airlines, such as easyJet and Ryanair in the UK, or Southwest Airlines in the USA, is due in part to the clarity with which they have been able to align their dominant brand value (low fares) with customer expectations. However, the long-term successes have also maintained other brand values, such as high punctuality and ease of booking.

Four expressions of brand

Why do people become so confused about brand? One significant reason is that organizations are themselves confused about where the brand rests and who it is aimed at. There are at least four ways in which the brand can be expressed, as indicated in Figure 7.1.

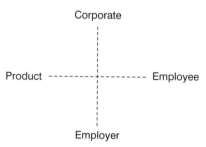

Figure 7.1 Four expressions of brand

Corporate brand expression relates to how the company is viewed by key external stakeholders, such as shareholders, the press, customers and major environmental influence groups. Sometimes, these same people may also be employees. Given the different viewpoints of, say, investors and environmentalists, maintaining a coherent brand statement at the corporate level is far from easy. Critical issues for the brand here include trust (is the company honest in what it says?), reliability/consistency (does it have a record of doing what it says it will? does it have a relatively smooth track record of growth or is it characterized by peaks and troughs?) and clarity of values (what does it stand for and how relevant are those values to the nature and style of business?).

Product brand expression relates to specific goods and services. Companies such as Proctor and Gamble or Unilever choose to place greater emphasis on branding the products than on branding the corporation, because the product is more directly relevant to the customer. Where a group places a greater emphasis on the corporate brand, there is the potential for conflict between the two. When building societies in the late 1980s and early 1990s decided to buy up estate agents, there was a serious conflict in many cases between the corporate brand (conservative and trustworthy, if very dull) and the brand of the new product (flashy cowboys). It is unlikely to have helped those societies, which relied upon account holders' loyalty to protect them from demutualization. On the other hand, it is relatively easy to maintain consistency in the individual product brand, because it is targeted at a less disparate audience, the customer. (In practice, of course, there is 'leakage' in terms of the perception of, for example, shareholders and employees. It was shareholders, for example, who emphasized the discrepancy between product brand and product reality in one of the UK's biggest high street retailers – a perception that resulted in the downfall of the chief executive.

Employer brand expression relates to the perception of current and potential employees about whether the company is a good place to work. Companies, such as British American Tobacco, which are in unpopular industries, can nonetheless attract and keep high calibre employees by screening out those, who have moral objections to working there, and by ensuring that they treat their employees exceedingly well in terms of salary, working conditions, development opportunities and the social environment. The argument for having a strong reputation as an employer (often referred to as the employer brand) is difficult to challenge. It has clear and direct connections to ease and quality of recruitment, employee retention and workforce motivation.

Delivering the employer brand is a lot more difficult than defining and marketing it, however. For example, the bad odour that now surrounds the term 'empowerment' is to a large extent the result of employers promising benefits in the working environment, which they could not or were not prepared to deliver. Whereas corporate and product brand expressions require close co-operation and integration between public affairs and marketing; the employer brand requires close co-operation between public affairs and human resources.

Finally, employee brand expression concerns the interaction between employees and the company values – how the employees' attitudes and behaviours reflect, support and reinforce the brand expectations of the various external audiences *and those of the internal audience itself*. In order to be effective at managing this aspect of brand, companies need to establish high consistency between:

- the values statement that typically goes with mission and vision (or, increasingly, replaces them)
- the other three expressions of brand: corporate, product and employer.

At first sight it might seem that the 'employee brand' is simply an element of the employer brand (the kind of people who elect to work here), or of the product brand (because employee behaviour is a key factor in the service offering), or of the corporate brand (because the behaviour and speculation of the leadership is closely linked to the business reputation.) It is precisely because it has such universal influence that it helps to view the employee brand as an expression in its own right. Moreover, the employee expression of brand is the key to aligning and integrating the other brand expressions into one coherent, credible, deliverable set of characteristics that constitutes the total business brand. No matter how well articulated the brand messages are, they achieve reality only through what people within the business do. Only when employees and leaders both live the brand and its values do brand aspirations and brand reality become one and the same.

The total business brand demands that the organization both recognizes the various brand expressions and establishes continuous dialogue between those who have ownership (or partial membership) of them. The aim of this dialogue is to ensure that all audiences – internal or external – accept and respect the organization for a shared and consistent set of values and differentiating characteristics.

Failure to create and sustain such consistency leaves employees bewildered and directionless. A good example of failure in this respect occurred at the induction day for graduate recruits at an international financial services company. The published corporate values were explicit – really important personal obligations (such as the marriage of a good friend) took precedence over an urgent work task. But the product values (as professionals, the job always comes first) were more commonly applied, in the limited experience the graduates had already had with the company. The message they took away was live with and make the best of inconsistency in values.

The impact of the employee aspects of brand is seen most dramatically when companies attempt to launch a new corporate or product identity. Recent examples include a company that advertised itself nationally as passionate about its products. The employees were at the centre of this identity, but little or no effort went into enabling them to *be* passionate. Whenever there is a gap between the identity a company claims for its people and the experience of people dealing with the company, it will impact the business negatively. By contrast, businesses where the employees do behave fully in line with the customer promise tend to thrive.

These same conflicts in brand expression can very easily occur between all the four areas we have described. Many organizations end up with a plethora of apparently conflicting brands, with the result that their identity is very confused – to the detriment of their positioning and reputation with both internal and external audiences. Among the key questions all organizations should ask themselves regularly about their brand are:

- *Where should the brand sit?* In a company with a single dominant product or products with very close affinities, it makes sense to focus on the corporate brand and ensure that the products reflect this. Where there are many products, each with strong brand recognition and different identities, attempting to impose a common corporate brand may undermine their market presence. A handful of companies – usually small and quirky, such as the computer services companies Poptel and Happy Computers, or the market research company Leapfrog – have chosen to centre their brand expression around the employer elements. They believe that their policies as employers will act as a significant differentiator that will both attract the highest calibre workforce and build client recognition. Wherever the core of the brand is sited, however, it will be undermined if the brand expressions do not reflect the same values and priorities.
- *Where will the greatest differentiation be achieved?* Companies like Poptel, Happy Computers and Leapfrog in the UK and Sol in Finland, have made a conscious decision about the personality they want their customers to see. Other companies, such as Ben & Jerry's and Patagonia in the USA and Body Shop and Benetton in Europe have similarly established a differentiating identity by linking their products and/or the corporate brand with social or environmental causes. In research we carried out into oddball companies in the late 1990s, it became clear that companies with distinct personality have a competitive advantage over those whose persona is bland and difficult to distinguish from the pack. Marketeers have been telling us this for years, but the solutions they propose are typically marketing solutions. In reality, sustainable differentiation comes about by changing factors deep inside the organization – its ways of thinking, its ways of making hard decisions and, most of all, its *underlying philosophy*. Truly differentiated companies see and react to the world differently to the norm. Changing the company name, the design on its trucks, premises and notepaper, and the customer promise is like spending a day in a makeover salon. You may emerge with a new look in face and hair, and a radically different wardrobe, but it does not take long for acquaintances to recognize that it is still the same you underneath! To put it another way *Brand definition gets weaker the vaguer the corporate personality.* Conversely, *The stronger the differentiating personality, the less need the company has to market itself.* (The more you stand out from the crowd, the less you

have to advertise your presence – a lesson exemplified in previous decades by the UK retailer Marks and Spencer, until it allowed its personality to be eroded.)

- *How well are the four brand expressions integrated?* If there is *any* conflict between the brand expressions, you have a problem of identity. It is like saying, 'Fred's a very kind man to his colleagues at work, but he beats his children'. An inconsistent brand perception, especially where one expression of brand is deeply negative, will detract from the whole.

Problems frequently arise when companies attempt to sustain brand values which are in conflict with business imperatives, such as a company whose corporate brand centres around providing excellent quality products but which faces the need to reduce materials costs, or whose external brand depends on delivering excellent customer service while financial pressure is forcing it to cut back on customer service staff. In some cases this tension can drive forward excellent innovations such as effective online handling of standard queries, but too often it simply results in obvious inconsistencies – 'listening' companies who keep customers on hold for as long as an hour before dealing with their enquiries, or supposedly 'quality' products produced from excellent designs but using shoddy materials.

Integrating the brand expressions may mean taking and implementing some very tough decisions. Are you prepared to drop a profitable product or area of activity, because its characteristics do not completely fit the brand? Will you remove very senior people, who have a track record of sales success, if aspects of their behaviour are contrary to the brand values? If the answer is no, then you are unlikely ever to achieve the level of brand differentiation you desire.

Managing the brand, therefore, requires an integrated and proactive approach, led by top management and incorporating high levels of collaboration between marketing, corporate communications, HR and employee communication. The internal communicator should take responsibility for gathering the feedback that identifies:

- The extent to which employees are willing and able to 'live the brand'
- The barriers that prevent them from doing so
- The extent to which they believe the leaders' behaviour exemplifies the brand values
- How well they believe the organization is living up to the brand
- The extent to which they see the four brand expressions as mutually supportive and non-contradictory.

Although brand management does involve – particularly in the brand design process – a high level of listening to external, and sometimes internal, audiences' perceptions, it is primarily a one-way communication process. It is also primarily an externally facing process. While companies are increasingly paying attention to ensuring that employees at least understand the corporate and/or product brands, they rarely put much continuing effort into understanding and managing the brand perceptions of employees. Yet creating dialogue on these issues is essential, if employees are to translate awareness into behaviour change.

Internal communicators can help HR and other functions plan the communication elements of the change programmes, which will bring the four brand expressions into line. They can also help top management articulate and demonstrate to the internal audiences that there really is only one brand, assuming that is the case. The message internally must, of course, be consistent with that given out externally, so there is also a great deal of liaison and checking to do with the externally facing functions.

When it comes to a re-branding campaign, the internal communicator can add value by ensuring that employee perceptions and behaviours are factored into the process at an early stage. They can make the case that, instead of being an add-on activity, funded grudgingly when the main expense of designing the new identity is completed, communication with the employees should be the starting point for identity change. From **item**'s experience, we can state categorically that *Corporate identity changes should NEVER be communicated to the external world until they have been accepted internally and employees have already begun to put those changes into action in their behaviours and the organization has learnt how to support them in doing so.* In practical terms, this might mean delaying the public announcement of identity change two years or more, until it is part of the operational reality, rather than an aspiration that will not reflect the true customer experience.

Finally, there is a role for the internal communicator in recognizing and intervening when different parts of the organization create initiatives that are likely to instil brand confusion. For example, an oil company's operations function launched a company-wide quality programme based upon a set of very sensible customer values. At the same time, the HR function was busily developing a set of behavioural values in support of the corporate brand. Although there were some similarities between these two values sets, there were also elements based on very different philosophical standpoints. Neither function would back down, so the compromise solution was to produce a third document that demonstrated the links between the two sets of values. Had there been an earlier intervention, the two initiatives could have been integrated and could have given substantial support to the brand. As it was, both were weakened by the sticking-plaster approach.

Brand management and the four pillars of communication

Brand management and communication management are inextricable linked. A brand is worth nothing if it is not communicated. Indeed, it cannot be said to exist unless it has taken root in people's minds. Different audiences may hold a very different brand perception. (Labour voters will have a different perception of the Conservative Party than Tory voters, to use a UK example; similarly, lifelong Democrats are likely to assign a very different brand to Republicans than lifelong Republicans. Floating voters may have a multitude of mixed perceptions.)

Effective brand management supports the four pillars in a number of ways. It influences clarity of purpose by simplifying what the company wants to stand for and providing a framework within which communication by the company reflects those values. Companies often get into difficulties of identity when they end up with more than one set of brand values – for example, one that emphasizes behaviours such as teamwork and integrity, and is intended mainly for internal consumption, and one aimed mainly at customers which emphasizes aspects of the products or services.

The more the four expressions of brand are allowed to have an independent existence, the more the company succumbs to the dysfunctions of multiple personality disorder.

Brand consistency demands that there is one set of core values that permeates the entire supply chain, from investors (the providers of capital) and suppliers (who we do business with and how) through employees to customers. That in turn implies a consistency of message which, as we have seen, is frequently absent.

The outcome of successful brand management is behaviour along the supply chain that aligns with the values. There are excellent examples of companies that have accepted investors only if they share core values. One Californian bank effectively made investors pass an interview to be allowed to join, for example. Furniture-makers have persuaded their suppliers to adopt values relating to the use of renewable forests; shoemakers to stop the use of whale oils in shoe leather. And marketers have for many years either adapted customer behaviour or sought specific groups of customers who share the same values. Some consumer businesses make this the centrepiece of their marketing strategy. Body Shop and record store Virgin Records, for example, focus heavily on building a bond of common interest between customers, employees and owners.

Jan Carlzon's famous concept of 'moments of truth' asserts in essence that every contact between an organization and its customers either reinforces or undermines the brand the company wishes to maintain. Behaviour that is merely congruent with the brand is largely unnoticed and has little effect, other than cumulatively to build expectations of what will happen. Behaviour that exemplifies the brand promise in ways the customer does not expect tends to reinforce it; behaviour that disappoints the customer undermines it. All of which is common sense. What is less obvious, however, is that moments of truth occur all the way along the supply chain. Brand dissonance – when the actual brand or reputation of the company is significantly at variance to the one it aims for – at *any* point on the supply chain can cause serious problems for the business, as we saw in the chapter on strategies for stakeholder communication.

Key questions here for the IC function, therefore, are:

- How do we help the organization achieve consistency of message about the brand values along the supply chain, when so much of the territory is owned by other functions, such as marketing or investor relations?
- How do we help create a credible link between the brand values and employee behaviours, given that employee behaviour is usually seen as the province of either HR or line management?

Of course, the IC function could say: 'This is none of our business, then. We'll provide practical help, for example in managing campaigns, when we are asked to and leave it at that.' The problem with such a stance is that it automatically relegates the function to a non-strategic role. To be involved in the crafting and development of strategy, the IC function needs to take a proactive stance that:

- identifies how employees perceive the brand(s)
- involves employees in discussing and planning how to make the brand a reality in the areas they can influence
- monitors internal behaviours against the brand values
- ensures that employees are aware of successes and failures in living the brand.

Trusting interfaces with customers are essential in building customer loyalty. They are also essential in ensuring that employees at all levels live the brand, because the behaviours that deliver the brand promise almost always include strong elements of teamwork and, often even more importantly, *inter-teamwork* – high levels of collaboration between teams. The vast majority of service quality failures (the negative moments of truth) occur not because of bad behaviour by an individual but because of failures of communication.

Consider the case of a highly successful European home entertainments company. It provides a high-quality product, but its brand was (and, at the time of writing, still is) frequently undermined by an inability to develop effective relationships between the call centre employees, who deal with customer queries and problems, and the service engineers, who make home visits. According to a call centre supervisor, at one stage the call centre staff and the engineers were not *allowed* to talk to each other. (This company also instituted a policy, whereby the director in charge of customer service refused to respond to phone calls from frustrated customers!)

The result is that customers may wait in all day for a visit that does not happen. In the absence of serious competition the brand dissonance does not matter too much, but in a more competitive environment the interface between the service engineers and the call centre staff would be critical in maintaining competitive advantage.

Trusting interfaces are established, most frequently and most successfully, through dialogue – through meaningful and open, exploratory communication that allows people to understand and value each other. Traditionally, the IC function has not played much of a role here. Communication within the team and between teams has been a matter for line managers. However, the brand and its associated values provide a basis for this kind of dialogue: a shared problem that demands discussion, collaboration and the development of shared solutions. The IC function can and should play a significant part in providing or stimulating the channels for communication within and between teams and in building the competence to generate trust.

Brand management needs effective and efficient systems of sharing information, for several reasons. For a start, the company needs to know:

- how customer perceptions of the brand are changing, especially in relation to competitors' brands

- how well the brand values are being enacted at the customer interface
- where the employees are experiencing difficulties in delivering the brand.

The first two of these issues are largely outside the remit of the IC function. However, employee perceptions of customer behaviours and attitudes are an important but frequently neglected source of brand management information. Very few companies make effective use of critical incident reporting (CIR), for example, where employees are encouraged to record instances where customers have shown pleasure or displeasure with the products or service they have received. Instead, they employ armies of market researchers, at great cost, to gather data which is far removed in time and place from the moment of truth. Critical incident reporting, by contrast, is inexpensive, continuous and immediate.

The IC function can also help identify problems in delivering the brand, from inadequacies in training, resources, supervisory leadership, or policies that conflict with the brand values. Creating forums, where employees can discuss such issues and suggest practical remedies is not just about continuous improvement; it is about constantly adapting the brand delivery process to the environment, both internal and external. To make this process work at its best, marketing information from external sources must be packaged into forms that are *meaningful* and *actionable* by the employees. Take a practical example. Staff at a building society were given information about the monthly variations in customer satisfaction. When satisfaction levels fell, top management expected the staff to discuss ways of presenting a more friendly, welcoming face to customers. The staff, however, placed the blame on additional backroom duties, which meant that there were less counter staff, which in turn meant longer queues and less time to be chatty with customers. An attitude of 'it's not our problem' soon developed.

By contrast, a competitor asked employees what information from marketing would be helpful to them in suggesting and making improvements. The staff in this case identified that the *time* customers came into the branch was an important factor. Accurate information about satisfaction levels at different times of day enabled them to design and implement, with management approval, work schedules that addressed the issues directly.

Top management communication behaviour should be influenced by the brand, because the leadership needs to be seen as the living embodiment of the brand values. A few organizations measure the brand behaviour of leaders from top to bottom of the

Table 7.1 Four expressions of brand

Key questions	Corporate brand	Product brand	Employer brand	Employee brand
	Clarity	*Clarity*	*Clarity*	*Clarity*
	How clearly do people understand what the organization 'stands for'?	How clearly is the customer promise explained to employees?	Do people inside and outside the company have a consistent and positive perception of its behaviour as an employer?	How clearly do employees understand what behaviours are expected of them? Do they accept these as appropriate?
	Trust	*Trust*	*Trust*	*Trust*
	Where do we most need to develop trust between people and functions?	Do employees themselves trust the product or service? (Do they recommend it to other people?)	Do employees believe the company delivers on its promises to them?	Do employees feel supported by each other and their managers in living the brand values?
	Information	*Information*	*Information*	*Information*
	What do people inside the company need to know to live the brand values?	Are employees sufficiently informed about customer expectations and concerns?	Are existing employees frequent and effective recruiting agents for the organization? Do they have the information they need to compare this employer with others?	Do employees receive (and give) meaningful and accurate feedback about performance in living the brand values?

	Brand ownership	Role of internal communication
	Top management Do employees believe that top management are truly committed to the brand values?	*Top management* Stimulate dialogue on how to put the corporate brand into practice Measure performance internally against the corporate brand
	Top management How passionate do employees believe top management is about the product brand?	*Marketing* Raise awareness of the product brand Help make it meaningful to employees in terms of their own roles
	Top management Are there effective channels to alert top management to concerns about the company's performance as an employer? Are these concerns demonstrably listened to?	*Human Resources* Help HR build and sustain dialogue with employees and measure changing perceptions
	Top management Does top management consistently recognize and reward employees' efforts to live the values?	*Line management* Help build dialogue between employees and all the other brand owners

organization as part of the overall management of culture change, but brand consciousness in the organization demands constant reinforcement from what top management says and does. When announcing a new investment or an acquisition, how does this support the brand promises? How do the visible signs of the organization fit with the brand? Walmart and IKEA, for example, both built their brands around frugality, from top management behaviour (economy-class travel) to very modest headquarters building and regional offices.

The role of the IC function here is one of intermediary between top management's good intentions and the reality of the perceptions of internal audiences. If employees perceive that top management does not walk the talk, or does not really take one or more of the brand values seriously, exhorting them to live the brand is a waste of effort. Internal communication can provide the measurement and feedback processes, help create opportunities for the leadership to talk from the heart to small groups of employees and ensure that the messages that come from the centre do not conflict with or confuse the values. (A classic case of the latter was the town council, which on the same day issued a newsletter from the CEO outlining a policy of empowerment, to support service values, and a memo from the finance function reducing the level of spending managers could authorize without permission from above.)

The internal communication function and management of the four brands

Table 7.1 shows how an effective communication strategy reinforces each of the four brands.

Managing brand inconsistency

When the four brands are not fully aligned, it takes effective communication strategies and practices, first, to identify the problems and, second, to facilitate the remedial processes. The remedies for any shortcomings or inconsistencies within any one of the brands may lie in more or better communication; but they may equally lie in changes of policy, reward systems or supporting infrastructure (e.g. the IT provision).

In the chapter on stakeholder communication, we established the value of measurement processes that tracked and compared the psychological contract between the organization and various audiences, both internal and external. The same principal applies to brand management. Each of the four brands can be measured in terms of how well it is being delivered. Each can also be compared with the others over time, to determine critical influences. For example, the Virgin Group of companies has historically had a very positive brand in terms of customer service and innovation. That reputation, heavily promoted by founder Sir Richard Branson, was largely built on products and services started from scratch, with employees recruited for the purpose. The employee brand was an important and highly positive part of the Virgin reputation. When Branson acquired a UK train operator, however, with the purchase came the existing staff. Decades of very different employee behaviours have been hard to change. The failure of the employees to live up to the corporate brand was made worse by service failures – in large part the result of problems with the rail infrastructure – which did no favours to the product brand. The extent, to which this catalogue of woes has damaged the corporate reputation remains to be seen, but the conflict between brands is one of the biggest challenges for the Virgin Group.

In situations such as this, the four pillars of communication again come into their own. The remedial strategy should include significant effort to:

- make expectations clear
- build trust between the organization and the acquired employees
- provide the information people need to make improvements
- demonstrate visible and consistent commitment by top management to aligning the four brands.

Internal branding

It would be remiss to conclude a chapter on the complexities of brand communication within the organization without reference to the increasing use of branding processes to facilitate specific change programmes (for which see Chapter 6, Communicating during radical change) and *functional reputation*. In a study for the CIPD (the professional body for both human resources and training and development) some years ago, **item** examined how the reputation of the HR function was affected by the quality of its communications. Among the conclusions of the study was that poor reputation management by HR severely affected its ability to perform. Some of the themes that emerged will by now sound familiar – problems with lack of trust between HR and employees, lack of clarity about how precisely HR contributed to the business goals, uncommunicative HR leadership and a lack of information both about people's requirements of HR and how well the function was fulfilling those expectations. Among the factors that contributed to a high reputation for the HR function was a structure that allowed frequent opportunities for impromptu dialogue between HR staff and line managers. MORI's studies have shown that in general a higher level of contact results in greater trust, proving that no department can afford to ignore the need to develop its visibility.

Since the study, we have run many one- and two-day seminars for senior HR professionals. A core element of these workshops is identifying the HR brand – what it is now and what it needs to be, if the function is to operate to its full potential within the organization. Another important task for the function which these workshops address is the need to recognize what action can be taken to improve visibility and perceptions of the department, including publicizing its past successes and proactively making suggestions as to what it can offer in the future.

Summary

The melting pot of the mixture of brands within an organization, and the need to achieve consistency of both message and action provides enormous potential for creativity and pragmatic innovation on the part of the employee communication function, in the role of process facilitator. After all, who else is better placed to measure how well managers and others are living the values, or how clearly defined the values are to different segments of the internal audience? And who is better equipped to stimulate the constructive dialogue that helps people throughout the organization identify brand inconsistency and develop ways of overcoming it?

This is not a role the internal communicator has traditionally played, yet it is, in our view, one that will become increasingly important as conflict between the four brand expressions becomes more obvious – an inevitability, given the increasing transparency of organizations to the internal and external observer through IT innovation. The ability to spot and tackle serious brand inconsistencies, and to sustain the total business brand, will become a significant competitive weapon in tomorrow's company.

Case study

Unisys

Unisys, the leading international e-business consultants, realized that to grow and evolve, it needed to develop change techniques that would improve its internal strategy.

Following the appointment of Brian Hadfield as Managing Director he announced his intention for Unisys UK to improve its service excellence – and the Vision ON project was born.

A project team was formed in April 2000, which set about making Unisys and its key elements the supplier of choice and employer of choice for encouraging a sense of ownership, providing a 'safe' environment for Unisys people to speak up, providing the best internal customer service experience, becoming the supplier of choice and the employer of choice, driving great ideas into reality and giving customers the sort of service they only dream about.

A defining principle for the project was that employees should understand that this was not an event or campaign but a programme of workshops, process improvements and communications designed to build a culture of exemplary customer service based on exceptional employee behaviour.

The company's goal was to create an environment where the total service ethos would thrive. The characteristics of such an environment included that:

- field staff have the skills, tools and encouragement to deliver exceptional service
- middle management understand the key drivers of a service climate and coach and actively support their staff to excel
- senior management embrace the vision as a coherent team, walk the talk and are actively leading the change programme.

Vision ON is based on four guiding principles which Hadfield is passionately committed to:

- creating customer experiences which inspire recommendation
- honouring our commitments
- doing the right thing
- working together at improving our work life.

In addition to enhancing client service, Vision ON embraced many aspects of Unisys work life and improved synergy between the internal groups.

The projects

After brainstorming sessions the Vision ON team revealed twenty projects that would be the base of all the changes needed. From this list three were chosen that would make a quick difference, possibly inside 100 days. The three were:

- *How can we make it easier to work in multi-business projects and help business units to co-operate and create a more unified Unisys?*
- *We know where we fail in providing service internally, to partners, and to our customers. By gathering the customer feedback we shall determine their expectations of best-in-class suppliers and be able to focus on their priorities for doing business.*
- *How do we recognize people who make a difference to service excellence? By focusing on reward and recognition we're going to change that!*

Suggestions

Vision ON could only be successful if the day-to-day problems were identified. Therefore, employee suggestions were extremely critical in dealing with all aspects of change. Every month employees were asked for specific suggestions relating to a particular theme.

All input responses were kept up to date on the web site. The suggestions medium revealed some of the occasional frustrations of corporate life but, most importantly, it resolved certain projects and raised other issues.

Suggestions boxes were located across the UK with input remaining anonymous unless the provider requested otherwise. Prizes were given each month for the best suggestions and almost 500 suggestions were submitted in the first six months.

Awards

Winners were selected each month for demonstrating one or more of the four guiding principles of Vision ON. This could be a team or individual effort.

The awards included a special commendation, lunch hosted by UK Managing Director Brian Hadfield and a poster campaign revealing the winners which is placed around all the UK sites.

The impact

Helen Love, Communications Director at Unisys, says:

After six months of patience and planning, the programme has worked to great effect. We are proud that our 8500 employees around the UK have

seriously become involved with Vision ON and ensuring its success. Vision ON has allowed employees the chance to either vent their frustrations or give constructive criticism. All employees are aware of what Vision ON is and what it has been implemented for – they understand that it's growing all the time and have seen the deliverables. Some of the remaining projects will come to a natural close while others will reform into different yet achievable problems. This is a rolling project, that we intend to improve our track record on, all the time.

M&A
(mayhem and
anarchy?)

Almost every article or book we have seen about merger and acquisition starts off with two claims. One is that most M&A projects do not deliver value to shareholders. The other is that there is really no such thing as a merger – only acquisitions – and that, however the acquirer dresses it up, they have the dominant position and will use it as they feel fit.

Both these statements are only partially true. Yes, the catalogue of failed acquisitions is very long. A well-known example is Quaker Oats, who bought Snapple in 1994 for $1.7 billion and sold it just three years later for $350 million. Consultants A.T. Kearney found that out of 115 mergers which took place between 1993 and 1996, 58 per cent did not add value, while Mercer Management Consulting put the figure at a startlingly similar 57 per cent.

Academic studies in general also support the notion that M&A is generally a bad move for the shareholders. In the 1980s, shareholders of acquiring companies generally reacted negatively to the news. In addition to the cost of a typical takeover premium (20–40 per cent), there are the costs of management time and attention diverted to other things. In view of the obvious disadvantages, it is no wonder sceptics have suggested that managers' motives for instigating mergers and acquisitions are often less than pure. Managers may, for example, overestimate their ability to manage acquired companies, pursue personal goals which are at odds with the interests of the shareholders or simply act out of a desire to emulate other companies who have made acquisitions.

Even if a merger begins with the best of intentions, managers and executives of both acquiring and acquired companies face a huge challenge as the secrecy which surrounds such deals makes it difficult for them to learn from the mistakes of their predecessors. Most research is conducted on the basis of retrospective assessments by managers, and agrees that one of the most common causes of failure is culture clash, yet one survey found that out of fifty-eight UK mergers, only fourteen had considered the cultural issues before the purchasing decision was made. Even where cultural factors are taken into consideration, there is no guarantee that they will be successfully managed. Another study, of almost a thousand managers in acquired companies, found that 90 per cent were unprepared for the changes in their status and the organization's structure which would result from the acquisition.

When two savings banks merged, the difference in culture resulted in immediate hostility between employees of the two companies. A year after the merger, former employees of the company whose culture had been replaced were significantly less satisfied and committed than employees of the company whose culture had been retained, despite the fact that before the merger they had been more favourable towards the change.

In one cross-border merger with which **item** was involved, we were given from 4 p.m. Friday to produce a newspaper in all the main local languages to be on people's desks at 9 a.m. on Monday. The merger has stuck, although there have been clashes between managers from different national cultures, especially in terms of leadership style. French managers expect to tell staff what to do in broad terms and then discuss the detail, UK managers question the fundamentals, while Germans have been described as 'saying yes and then doing whatever they want'.

The common factor to most, if not all of these, is that they are in essence issues of communication. A study in 1996, which looked at 350 mergers and acquisitions in Europe, found that 75 per cent thought that communication planning was the main area that had not been given enough attention.

Indeed, surveys of M&A activity almost always identify communication as one of the areas, which top management feels is among the least well managed. In our research for *Transforming Internal Communication* (Kernaghan, Clutterbuck and Cage, 2001), we found that, although supporting major change programmes was one of the most significant activities to the internal communication department, it was viewed as far more important than successful.

But, if it is true that most mergers and acquisitions do not deliver the goods, why do so many companies persist in acquiring? Are CEOs generally so stupid that they keep banging their head against the M&A brick wall, when they know it hurts? And how does one explain the existence of so many high-performing groups of companies, across so many sectors? Part of the answer is supplied by a recent report in the *Academy of Management Journal* (Vermeulen and Barkema, 2001), whose authors argue that the process of ingesting new people and new ideas is essential to organizations' survival and that the upheaval of acquisition or merger provides a much needed stimulus. Assessing M&A activity solely on financial criteria is inadequate, they argue, especially in the short term.

Abuse of acquiror power is often referred to as 'Conqueror Syndrome'. Yet there are cases where companies are acquired precisely because of the strength of their management, who then assume dominant positions in the acquiring company. There are also enough examples of companies, which have managed the integration process so sensitively that power issues are not allowed to interfere.

There are some major implications in both of these sets of assumptions for the employee communication function. First, what you believe impacts what you do and the sincerity with which you do it. If you believe that the primary measure of an acquisition is its ability to create greater value than the two entities had on their own, the probability is that that is how you will justify the purchase. If the promised synergies take longer to take effect (or do not happen at all), you now have to deal with disbelief, demotivation and increased cynicism from employees. Given the statistics on value-creation above, this outcome is more likely than the more optimistic scenario!

If you genuinely believe that a merger is a marriage of equals, then you had better start behaving that way from day one. It only takes one or two peremptory memos or disrespectful comments from managers in the acquiring company to build negative expectations among employees in the acquired company. If the acquiring company managers see themselves as conquering heroes who have come to show their counterparts how to do things properly, no amount of dissembling will prevent these attitudes showing through to both sets of employees. Very quickly, people in more junior management positions will start to behave as 'lords of the manor' or 'rebellious serfs', depending which side they are on! One of the most demanding and difficult tasks for the internal communication professional is persuading top management not to think or behave in ways that will give an inapt message!

Second, people's previous experience will influence strongly their expectations this time around. Consider this example from a factory manager:

> This is the fourth new owner we've had in five years. The only similarity between the previous three is that they've all told us to cut costs. We know that we've cut just about everything, including people, that won't jeopardize our survival. People are just waiting for the axe to fall.

Understanding how these preconceptions will affect receptivity to messages from the acquiror is vital in managing the relationship with these employees. In the event, the new owners made no announcements for two weeks, while they listened to employees' concerns. They realized that any mention of cost-cutting would assume a great significance in employees' minds. So they focused instead on increasing sales and asked for people's involvement in improving service in ways that did not add to costs. Given a new perspective, the employees actually identified a whole range of savings, without actually looking for them. The company also made a big point of identifying the points of excellence in the factory – expertise that was as good or better than elsewhere in the enlarged group – and turned these people into ambassadors of what was good about the operation.

Third, as we saw in the introduction to this book, the psychological contract between employee and the company hinges to a large extent on the notion of creation of value *for all stakeholders*. Communicating the rationale for a merger solely or primarily from a shareholder perspective is akin to saying that it does not matter what employees think or feel about it. This may well be top management's attitude, of course, and it is certainly an opinion we have heard expressed more than once. However, a more perspicacious CEO will recognize the importance of gaining the willing commitment of a much wider audience. Even if the message to employees is not good news – for example, that the merger will mean major job losses – better to be upfront with this information and discuss the impact on the psychological contract openly, than leave the real discussion to the rumour mill and Friday night bar talk.

Why is major structural change so traumatic?

Not all acquisitions come with an implied threat. Much depends on the intent of the acquirer, in terms of both structure and purpose. Table 8.1 illustrates who is most likely to be affected by different circumstances of acquisition. In some cases and for some people, the change is likely to be seen more as an opportunity than as a threat – for example, where a company is acquired for the strength of its management team, or where the acquisition follows a long period of decline and paralysed management.

When a large and ailing retailer was acquired, the new ownership found that instead of being resentful, employees were keen for change, and typical feelings among line management were:

- For goodness' sake tell us who our boss is.
- Get rid of the excessive bureaucracy.
- Allow us to manage without too many people telling us what to do.
- We accept that there have to be redundancies, but select people on the grounds of age and incompetence and improve the terms.
- Tell us what you want to do and we'll get on with it.

In these circumstances, all the acquiring company has to do is avoid dissipating the goodwill generated by the change.

When M&A and other forms of major structural change are traumatic, it is because they create fear and uncertainty. Figure 8.1 shows one way of viewing the stages of emotional response to change, and how reactions can be altered as a result of the support provided (Klasen and Clutterbuck, 2002).

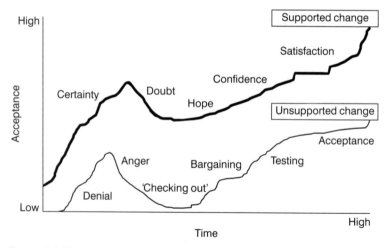

Figure 8.1 The stages of emotional response to change

Table 8.1 Who is impacted by acquisition?

Strategic intent	Style of ownership			
	Laissez-faire: Management by financial control	Strategy control	Integration of key functions	Complete integration
Entering new markets	Mainly senior managers	Mainly senior managers	Some employees at all levels	Everyone
Reducing costs through economies of scale	Everyone	Mainly senior managers	Some employees at all levels	Everyone
Sharing knowledge/expertise	Mainly key professionals	Managers and key professionals	Everyone	Everyone
Freeing up assets/cash generation	Everyone	Everyone	Everyone	Everyone
Securing supply	Senior managers	Senior managers	Mainly senior managers	Everyone
Increasing market share	Senior managers	Senior managers	Sales and marketing	Everyone
Increasing management depth	Top managers	Top managers	Top managers	Top managers

Comparisons have also been made between the psychological response to a merger or acquisition and a bereavement or loss. Employees involved in unwelcome changes react by passing through four stages:

1 Disbelief and denial.
2 Anger, rage and resentment.
3 Emotional bargaining.
4 Acceptance.

The fact that change has been accepted does not mean that employees are committed to the changed organization. They may accept that the changes have occurred while remaining fearful, unhelpful or even obstructive. Not surprisingly, studies have shown that in an uncertain working environment employees are more likely to be absent and to consider quitting. Job satisfaction and performance are also commonly affected.

Support is required at this stage as much as any other to maintain the changes to the organization. Companies undergoing change need to keep employees informed. Information must be provided promptly, before the rumour mill takes over. Communications must be accurate and credible, and should explain the rationale for changes as they occur.

A study published in *Training & Development* journal confirmed many of the negative consequences of failing to communicate. The study questioned employees of a large manufacturing and research firm less than a month after the sale and again three months later. In the intervening time, the company had discontinued its communication programme.

In the first survey, those employees who gave positive evaluations of the communication programme were more likely to perceive themselves as having some control over their personal situation, to be more committed to the organization and to be more satisfied with their jobs. They were less likely to intend to quit and had lower expectations of absenteeism. At this stage, employees were most likely to discuss changes with co-workers and family members, followed by immediate supervisors, non-work friends and upper management. In the second questionnaire, after the company's communication programme had ended, they were most likely to talk to co-workers, then family members. Supervisors were only as popular a choice as friends away from work and, once again, top management were the least likely choice. Since at both stages supervisors were a more popular choice than management, it is important for communicators to support team leaders, supervisors and line managers in providing the answers to employees' questions as far as possible. If it is genuinely impossible to provide the information employees seek, managers should be encouraged to explain the reasons why and estimate when the information will be available.

Typically, questions to which employees seek answers include:

- Will I still have a job?
- Will my subordinates still have a job?
- Will this still be the kind of company I want to work for?
- How will the change affect my status?
- How will my job content change?

While there will always be concerns about the negative effects of the change, there may also be the expectation of positive change. One retailer was surprised to discover that employees welcomed the prospect of a new employer when the company was acquired. They had been unhappy with the company's poor performance for some time and welcomed the prospect of new management turning it around.

One study compared two plants in a company undergoing a merger. Employees in one plant received only the level of communication typical of the company at the time – a letter from the CEO announcing the merger, followed by their usual weekly meetings with supervisors to discuss work issues. Following the merger announcement, the other plant carried out an extensive communication programme including:

- a twice-monthly merger newsletter detailing organizational changes and answering questions
- a hotline to a personnel manager to answer questions about organizational changes (based on regular updates provided by the vice-president of HR)
- a weekly meeting between the plant manager and the supervisors and employees of each department to address changes which specifically affected that department.

In addition, the plant manager continued the usual monthly meetings, and employees met weekly with their supervisors to discuss work issues.

Shortly after the merger announcement employees at both plants were asked about various aspects of their work, and personnel records were examined for data on absenteeism and turnover. Initially there was no difference between the two plants – both sets of results had declined compared to pre-merger levels. Later surveys, which took place after the communication programme was put in place at one plant, showed that the communication at first stabilized the results, and then improved them. Two months after the merger announcement, the plant with the communication programme had almost returned to pre-merger levels, while the other plant's results showed a continued decline.

So what do people have to be worried about? One of the most useful tools in the **item** armoury is the Worry Index – a simple checklist that helps organizations assess where employees concerns are deepest (Table 8.2). We have found that the degree to which people receive messages is a good indicator as to how

Table 8.2 The Worry Index

Security
Am I going to be made redundant, either now or in the future?
How many other people will be made redundant?
What are the terms on offer?
If I remain, how secure is the job and will my conditions face reduction?
If I am made redundant, will I be able to get another job?

My job
Will I get a new boss, and if so, will I like him or her?
Who will assess me?
Will I have to change jobs or work harder?
Will I have to work with different people?
Will I have to relocate?
How will my performance be measured?
If I have to make decisions, will I be able to cope?
With all this going on, will I be able to take my holiday as planned?

My prospects
Will this affect my status?
Will it reduce/enhance my chances of promotion?
Will I learn new skills?
Is this my opportunity to show what I can really do?
What do I get out of it?
If I learn new skills, will those skills help me get another job if I need to?

My values
Is this the company I thought I was working for?
What's happened to the caring attitude of the old company?
Do my contribution and loyalty count for nothing?
Will the company respect my home life?
Will I be happy if they move me out of my team?

Table 8.2 *continued*

Management motives
What does my boss think?
Can I trust the reasons they're giving me?
Will they treat us differently?
Is this just the tip of the iceberg?
Are they doing this to get rid of me?
They've screwed up, haven't they?
Are management going to change or just expect us to?

My beliefs
Why should we need to change when we're already successful?
Will they cut the dead wood around here?
What I do is OK – the changes won't apply to me, will they?
Will the changes they promise actually happen?
People won't stand for it, will they?
Why should I improve my performance when it's the management at fault?
We may have to change to keep the customers happy, but who's going to
    change things to keep me happy?
Why should I change my way of working just so the bosses can get rich?

The change
How am I supposed to understand what's required?
Have they thought this through?
Who's in charge?
How will they decide what to change?
When will it happen?
When is it supposed to be finished?
How many more changes are we going to have around here?
Will they keep me informed in future?
What about the changes I need to make me happier?
How will I know if the change is working?
Are they going to make time for us to make all these changes?

much change will actually take place. More than anything, people want answers to the questions that affect them and to deal with their anxieties and issues. When an organization understands what the issues are, it can understand a group's frame of reference and address it to establish a basis for communication.

What makes the problem worse in many cases, is the difference between what top management intends to say and what employees hear. Cynicism is likely to be very high during the period of highest uncertainty. Table 8.3 is a (only slightly) tongue-in-cheek interpretation of how employees may interpret messages from the top.

Table 8.3 A lexicon of acquisition double-speak

We wouldn't have bought your company, if we didn't think you were great – We could only afford the company because it was so badly managed

There's no need to worry about losing your job – We want you to go in our time, not yours/I'm not worried about losing my job

Everyone has the same opportunity to compete for jobs – It's all sewn up, but we're going through the motions

There are tremendous synergies between the two businesses – The finances don't add up

We have a clear vision of the future – We have some half-baked ideas, and we're winging it/We've lost the plot

We intend to invest in this business – We're going to have to cut the salary bill to fund changes

We share the same values – The new management cares about people issues even less than the old one

There's a wealth of opportunity out there – If there were, we wouldn't need your company

We've built a united team at the top – We've buried the hatchet for the moment

It will be business as usual – Until we work out where we're going to slash and burn

We'll clear up the uncertainties as soon as we can – We've got more important things to worry about

This will benefit us all – I've got my stock options

This will be a marriage of equals – To the victor the spoils

Knowing what to expect helps to reduce the worry level. It is easy to cope with a situation where you have a good understanding of what is likely to happen and where you have no reason to feel that you will be greatly disadvantaged by it. Where you know what is going to happen and you do not like it, you can at least take steps to deal with the issue – even if it is only to start looking for a new job! Where uncertainty is high, even if the level of negative impact is likely to be low, you may still invest it with higher significance (Figure 8.2). Where both uncertainty and potential impact are high, the employee may well become paralysed in indecision, unable to focus on what is important for the present, because of the black clouds in the future.

Uncertainty also has an impact on the psychological contract, the usually unwritten set of expectations between employee and

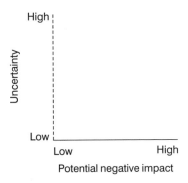

Figure 8.2 Uncertainty versus impact

employer. Will the existing contract be kept, or are all parts of it up for grabs? Where the psychological contract is clear, even if it is not seen by employees as fair and just, it is relatively easy for both sides to come to an accommodation about what each gives and receives. The contract usually evolves from a sense of transaction (exchanging A for B) to one based on a more subtle set of recognition, favours and indirect 'gifts'. For example, employees may work extra hours unasked to meet an urgent customer need, or the company may spontaneously relax dress codes.

Radical upheaval, or the prospect of it, throws all these accommodations into touch. Caution replaces trust as people recommence the delicate process of social negotiation, testing bit by bit what are the new expectations on each side. The relationship between employee and employer effectively starts again at the transaction end of the transaction – accommodation dimension.

Managing the M&A communication process

Like most complex tasks in business, managing the communication of merger and acquisition is a multifaceted task. The volume of work and the length of time, which the communication process will need, depend on the scale of the impact on the organization

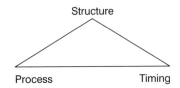

Figure 8.3 Core elements of communication management in M&A

and its employees. The simplest way to approach the communication management issues is to divide them into three core elements as in Figure 8.3.

Structure is about who is involved and in what capacity. Process is about the communication activities and how they are linked together. Timing is about what should happen when.

The structure of M&A communication with employees

When an acquisition or merger is announced, employees who have become inured to such changes often just shrug their shoulders. There may be no immediate response, but what certainly does happen is an explosion of informal, indirect communication. The initial instinct of many managers is to attempt to *control* communication. They monopolize the formal media, parcel out information only when they are sure it is safe to do so (which usually means it is vetted by committee, cauterized by lawyers and far too late to have any positive impact) and expect to influence employee opinion and emotion by *ex cathedra* statements. All these instinctive reactions have exactly the opposite effect to that intended.

Informal communication and dialogue between all those involved in or affected by the changes are in reality the cornerstones of effective M&A communication. People need space to air their concerns, to come to terms with what the change means to them and their colleagues, and to feel that they are being listened to. The more that top management encourages and participates in this informal debate, the more easily people will get behind the change and focus on helping to make it happen with least pain.

The informal debate takes place in a wide arena, much of it beyond the reach of top management anyway. For example, speculation in the press will fuel discussion about the wisdom of an acquisition, or the strategy behind it. Formal denials may help, but they may equally be seen as confirmation by the cynical, unless there is a strong track record of veracity and openness from top management.

The structure of M&A communication with employees therefore needs to be built around a number of key principles:

- The role of the internal communication function is to *inform* discussion, not to *manage* it.
- Integration of messages to stakeholders inside and outside the organization is essential.
- The communication team is everybody, although a core

communication team is essential to ensure that information is available (not just from the company to the employees, but vice versa and between employees of the two organizations).

Figure 8.4 illustrates how a typical good practice M&A communication team is structured.

Although their attention may be heavily focused on the

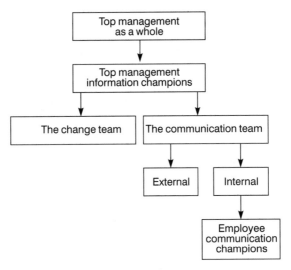

Figure 8.4 Structure of M&A communication

financial and logistics aspects of the deal, top management *have* to be visibly and actively involved if the communication process is to have credibility. While the communication team is only part of the larger M&A team, top management must at the same time see themselves as part of the communication team. One way of dealing with this complexity is to make two or three executives, including the CEO, spokespersons for top management as a whole. However, it is essential that every member of the top management team is fully briefed and emitting exactly the same messages as the spokespersons. Communication issues therefore need to be on the agenda whenever they meet. It may also be appropriate to provide a daily bulletin on communication issues so that they are all acquainted with what should and should not be said, and so that they understand the immediate concerns of each of the key stakeholder audiences.

The change team (or merger management team) will involve people from a variety of disciplines who may not have worked together on a high-pressure task before. They will almost certainly have communication issues between the members, so there is a significant role for the communication function in helping them manage these. (There will probably not be enough time to work through all the stages of forming, storming, norming and performing during the lifetime of the project.) It is essential to have at least one experienced employee communication professional in the change team.

The M&A communication team is where internal and external messages (both to and from top management) are aligned. There is inevitably some conflict here, especially when the company is quoted on the Stock Exchange. Stock Exchange regulations may make it difficult to inform employees before shareholders, yet the last thing the company normally wants is for employees to hear such news through the media. Good practice seems to be have a small core team, some of whom also take responsibility for communicating to other colleagues in the communication function. The communication plan is developed in this group and fleshed out in detail in the separate public affairs and internal communication teams.

Employee communication champions – typically managers across the business, who accept the responsibility to be the local mouth, ears and eyes for the communication function – are also an essential part of the structure. They need frequent exposure not just to the facts, but to the broader thinking of top management and the change team. While constant e-mail briefings may help, they also need face-to-face meetings (in person or by video-conferencing) to absorb the flavour of change.

How extensive the internal communication team needs to be will depend upon the impact of the acquisition. A large company acquiring a much smaller entity, which it intends to leave pretty much alone, does not need much of a communication structure at all. A merger of equals, by contrast, will need a great deal.

The protracted nature of negotiations and establishing the integration plan often means that two, parallel merger communication structures emerge – one in each company. The sooner these can be integrated, the sooner the uncertainties will be tackled and the smoother the acquisition or merger will proceed as a whole. Two cases, both from the financial services industry, illustrate how *not* to do it.

Case one involved the merger of two large financial retailers. One had a very stiff, bureaucratic culture; the other a more entrepreneurial, open culture. As merger talks progressed, and once the initial announcements were made, employees in the more bureaucratic culture found that they could learn more about what was going on by calling friends and acquaintances in the more open company, than they could through any form of internal communication. Although the bureaucratic company was the larger partner, the emphasis its top management placed on 'need to know' was one of the factors that eventually resulted in many of them losing out in the jobs race as the merger was consummated – to the extent that it almost became a reverse takeover.

In the second case, top management in the acquired company was so paranoid about maintaining their independence, that they made it a punishable offence for staff – even at a fairly senior level – to contact their opposite numbers in the acquiror without specific permission. As the top team were not particularly good conduits of information from the new parent company, relatively little information made it through to employees and rumours multiplied unchecked. When top management did make statements, they were regarded with suspicion. Motivation and performance plummeted. All of this got in the way of the broader acquisition objectives, making it more difficult to obtain the investment the acquisition needed. The downward spiral continues at time of writing.

In **item**'s experience, the process for integrating the two teams needs to be established from the start. Key issues to consider are:

- Who are the counterparts in each area and how can they best work together? (Job roles are unlikely to be exactly the same in both companies – for example, what is a full-time internal communication role in one may be a mixed IC and public relations (PR) role in another.)
- How will the combined team reach a consensus on the messages it sends out?
- Who else has to sign off those messages (e.g. the two CEOs) and how will the team ensure that it does not get caught between conflicting views of what should be said?
- What is the procedure for reacting to queries or concerns in a specific area?
- What media can be shared and what need to be created/used separately?

One company undergoing a merger provided an excellent opportunity to begin integration, by sending teams of employees from each company to brief a group within the other company. The briefers were trained by the PR department and had prepared answers to all the anticipated questions. When unanticipated questions arose, they consulted top management in order to provide an authoritative answer. In addition to improving relations between the two companies during the merger, the process improved managers' communication competence and resulted in improvements in their own job performance as well as employees' morale.

Role of the internal communication professional

During the course of a merger or acquisition, the communication professional can help in three key areas:

- identifying and managing cultural differences between the two companies
- developing a coherent communication plan and campaign
- advising top management on what to say and when.

By managing cultural differences between the companies, the communicator can reduce potential conflict between the two teams, leaving management free to focus on growing the business. Valuable tools for studying the cultures of the two organizations include:

- former employees
- friendly headhunters
- company literature
- press coverage.

If there is a reasonable fit and employees of both companies are aware of the fact, then most people will rapidly accept the change. If there is not a good fit, then problems can be eased by giving the acquired company as much autonomy as possible, although this reduces the benefits of synergy between the organizations.

In either case, the communication plan can do much to assist the process of acceptance. In particular, the internal and external stories should be consistent. An **item** survey found companies took three main approaches to integrating internal and external communications:

- circulating press releases and internal announcements in parallel
- setting up steering committees
- routing all communication through the directors.

Timing is also critical as rumour is always rife at times of change, and more so if official information is not immediately forthcoming (Table 8.4).

Table 8.4 Timing of M&A communication with employees

When	Key objectives	Key questions for acquiring company	Key questions for acquired employees	Key messages to acquired employees	Key messages to current employees	Media criteria
Day 1	Reassurance; recognize and acknowledge concerns; align internal and external communications	How can we make an immediate positive impression?	Why? What's going to happen?	Rationale – we know what we are doing; our motives are pure; broad scope of the likely change; why you should trust us	Rationale – we know what we are doing; this will/will not affect you; broad scope of the likely change	Fast; broadly aimed; open; straightforward; mainly one way; segment by audience
Week 1	Overcoming uncertainty; achieving a sense of purpose and direction; focus on the future; understand concerns of each key audience segment	How much can we balance the employees' need for clarity and explicit information against our need to keep options open? How can we balance making the changes happen against being available to explain them?	What is going to be the impact on me and my unit? Will I still have a useful role? Who are these people? What do they stand for?	There is a plan; where structural change will and will not make a difference; this is a good company to work for; these are our values; clearer picture of scale of likely changes; what we value you for; we hope to learn from you and vice versa; headlines of culture change needed	There is a plan; these are your new colleagues; this is how they fit into our future; clearer picture of likely changes and how they will be affected	Need for discussion and dialogue; visible management; feedback and rumour management; emphasis on face to face, supported by other media; symbolic gestures; be seen to listen and respond

Continued overleaf

When	Key objectives	Key questions for acquiring company	Key questions for acquired employees	Key messages to acquired employees	Key messages to current employees	Media criteria
Month 1	Looking forward; reinforcing sense of positive purpose and mutual respect/values; continue to manage uncertainty	How can we retain credibility? Are the messages getting through?	How long will the uncertainty last? What should I be doing differently?	Things are starting to happen; clearer explanation of intended changes and their implications; discomfort is essential but temporary	Things are starting to happen; clearer explanation of intended changes and their implications	Branding major change; communicating by example; 'plugging in' the change team – ensuring continuous information; feedback and rumour management; draw down, not pour down; quality versus quantity of information; frequent short meetings versus fewer long meetings; continuous feedback
Quarter 1	Reinforce commitment to change; overcome acquisition fatigue	Are people committing to the changes? Where are the main pockets of resistance? How can we sustain interest?	Is anything really happening? Are the rumours true? When is it all going to get back to normal?	How the planning is progressing; how you can contribute to the discussions; timescales	How the planning is progressing; how you can contribute to the discussions; timescales	Recognition and praise for 'right' behaviour
Year 1	Celebrate progress so far; put the past firmly behind	What can we learn for next time?	Is it really over? What happens next?	Thank you; apologies for the discomfort and disruption; vision of the future	Thank you; apologies for the discomfort and disruption; vision of the future	Wide mix of media

Key processes in M&A communication with employees

The following are some of the communication processes which can add credibility to the success of M&A activity.

Communication due diligence

Due diligence is a vital part of the M&A process. As the authors of an *Academy of Management* article on the subject (Marks and Mirvis, 2001) point out, it should go beyond the financial aspects of the merger or acquisition, to consider the 4 Ps:

- purpose
- partner
- parameters
- people.

In other words, they must consider the arguments for and against the deal in terms of the need that it is intended to meet, the suitability of the company selected to meet that need, and the operational parameters which might influence the deal, as well as human aspects such as the mindsets of both senior teams and the willingness of employees to change. According to the authors, up to twenty people can be required to complete the process thoroughly, and one company even went as far as to create two due diligence teams to ensure that nothing was overlooked in their enthusiasm for the potential deal.

Communication, like diligence, also examines the capability of the target organization to communicate effectively during the critical phases of the transition's new ownership. Key questions include:

- Does it have effective systems to reach all employees and other stakeholders rapidly?
- How credible will employees perceive communication about the merger/acquisition from their top management/from our top management?
- How is the internal communication function viewed by people in the target organization?
- How will the communication professionals fit with our team and our culture?

Communicate from the employee perspective

Understanding the attitude and the level of receptivity of the employees in both organizations is critical in getting the right tone and style of communication. Making the effort to listen to employees before attempting to send them messages about the merger or acquisition gives you the reflective pace to consider how best to engage them. While the initial announcement may not have the luxury of consultation with employees – it should keep very distinctly to the bare facts – dialogue with employees can start very shortly afterwards in most cases.

Attitudes towards the other side will play a major role in the style of communication the leaders adopt. Where there is low regard between these two companies, people in the acquirer organization are likely to be resistant to dialogue, at least initially. The acquirer needs to adjust its own attitudes and demonstrate good intuition to a more consultative style. Where one party has high regard for the other, consultation is likely to build bridges and change attitudes (Figure 8.5). And where both have high regard for each other, consultation can turn more rapidly into participation. Part of the internal communicator's job is to help move *both* organizations into this more positive, proactive communication environment – by building trust, sharing information, helping top management demonstrate supportiveness and helping clients understand what the acquirer intends to do.

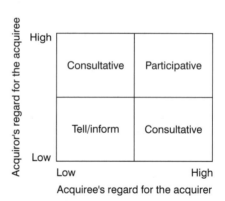

Figure 8.5 Communication style versus terms of respect

People's receptivity will also be affected by their concern about the outcomes of the change (Figure 8.6). The combination of fear and a perception that the acquiring organization has very different values, which the employee does not endorse, is likely to lead to high levels of mistrust and very low receptivity. Fear, combined with an acceptance that the values of the acquiring organization are positive, will typically lead to acceptance, for the greater good, but personal concerns will moderate the level of receptivity. Equally, receptivity will be moderate if the employee feels guilty about publicity from a bad situation – i.e. when the outcome may be good but they have little faith in the acquiring organization. Ideally, of course, the employee will be enthusiastic about both the outcomes and the values of the organization they are joining – in which case receptivity will be very high.

Perception of outcomes:		
Desirous: high expectation, things will work out well for me/my colleagues	**Guilt** 'Do I really deserve this?' Moderate receptivity	**Enthusiasm** 'Tell me more!' High receptivity but may be impervious to messages about the downsides/risks
Fearful: high uncertainty; expectation that things will work out badly for me/my colleagues	**Bloody-minded** 'Go away!' Low receptivity	**Martyrdom** 'For the greater good' Moderate receptivity
	Low High	
	Alignment of values and beliefs	

Figure 8.6 Perception of outcomes versus alignment of values and beliefs

Recognizing the differences in receptivity enables the internal communication professional to adjust the messages and the media over time. Gradually building bridges is a lot faster in the medium rather than blundering in with the wrong message or the wrong style!

Minimize uncertainty and rumour

Fears about job losses create the most anxiety, but that anxiety can be managed. Companies who had undergone mergers said that next time they would plan for more continuous communication. Event-driven communication makes for a lot of uncertainty as employees fill in the gaps with rumour. Gaps in information also result in people assuming a hidden agenda. If you are temporarily unable to provide information, at least explain why and, if possible, when the information will be available.

Allow for the fact that face-to-face communication is particularly situational, and managers under pressure and uncertain about their own futures are not in the best situation for delivering effective communications. Mergers and acquisitions are a stressful time for everybody and may expose big gaps between a company's belief about its ability to communicate, and the realities of the situation.

Stakeholder management

By their very natures, mergers and acquisitions enlarge the corporate constituency. Communication becomes more complex, requiring a high degree of integration, co-ordination and sensitivity to reflect the different – even multiple – relationships each stakeholder has with a company. In this way the contradictions, confusion and embarrassments which have been known to derail mergers and acquisitions can be avoided.

Communication needs to take place in parallel to internal and external audiences. This is especially crucial in companies where some or all employees are also customers or shareholders. However, even where there is less overlap between stakeholder groups, if internal communication is made the Cinderella, dissatisfaction and demotivation will follow.

Whoever is chosen as the co-ordinating point needs to apply a range of questions to each audience. These include:

- To what extent will the merger/acquisition affect this audience positively or negatively?
- What potential do they have to influence the business directly or indirectly, positively or negatively?
- How likely is it that the effects of our action on one group will prompt a response – possibly unfavourable – from another?

Communication symbols

At times of uncertainty, employees will be scrutinizing management's actions more closely for signs of what the future holds. It is more important than ever to consider how you can use symbols to lower resistance, re-energize staff and shift their focus to the imperatives of the future.

You can help by listening to what employees did not like about the past. Putting it right could be the 'What's in it for me' factor essential to winning over sceptical employees. One company found that an improved share scheme was the key to motivating staff after a takeover, but the incentive need not be financial. We have seen everything from enhanced canteen facilities, to repainted buildings and new bike sheds contribute to successful change.

It's also important to recognize what has successfully determined the company's culture in the past and to make a conscious decision about what needs to be retained (Table 8.5). Cultural differentiators may include the building (modern or traditional), social and educational backgrounds of the senior team, the terms of compensation and benefits. In addition, there are more

Table 8.5 Learning about each other – some key questions

Awareness

What are the demographics of each company?
What are each company's core values?
Core operating principles (e.g. centralized or decentralized)?
How have the companies dealt with other acquisitions?
How long is the acquisition/integration process going to last?
How will the companies fit with each other?
Who are the key players?

Understanding

What changes can we expect in:
- The size and structure of the organization?
- Core values?
- Core operating principles?
- Key personnel?
- The jobs of ordinary people?
- The way we are recognized and rewarded?
- Leadership style?
- How the company invests in people?
- The strategy for the business?

Will there be other, similar acquisitions?
What are the personal values and priorities of the key players?
Where are the points of greatest potential friction in the culture and market emphasis?
How will the merger be handled?
- How will people be assessed for merged jobs?
- How will people who lose out be treated?
- Will it be a short, sharp shock or a long drawn out process?

Who is more likely to win/lose in the integration process?
What role can I play?

Commitment

What fears and concerns do people have?
Are these being addressed effectively and with sensitive segmentation?
What involvement do people have in influencing the changes that are going to happen?
What procedures are there to ensure people have sufficient time to come to terms with each change before it is implemented?
Is people's 'sense of being valued' being reinforced or undermined?
How capable and competent do they feel to handle these changes?
Where are the role models for them in surviving and thriving on change? Are these role models appropriate?
To what extent do people trust/distrust the merger/acquisition partner (corporately and as individuals)?

personal factors such as the people in each culture who are highly regarded, their backgrounds and roles. Is one company oriented strongly around financial goals while the other places the focus on social responsibility or being an employer of choice? In addition to helping decide whether the venture is appropriate, an understanding of these issues will help to avoid potential conflict if it goes ahead.

Employees will also look to the treatment of leavers as a symbol of the merged company's attitude to its staff. There will be a great deal of curiosity about the decision as to who remains and who departs, and as to the package offered. The selection process can be used as a powerful demonstration of the new company's values, or it can degenerate into a demoralizing battle for the remaining posts. Depending on how they are treated, departing employees can become ambassadors for the company, or stir up considerable resentment among those who remain. The whole process provides strong indications to employees of how the company will operate going forward – make sure they are the right ones.

Managing rumour mills

One of the key elements in minimizing rumours is developing sufficient trust so that people feel they can ask directly for any information they require. Reducing uncertainty – releasing any information you can, and being clear about why other information cannot be released and when it will be available – is also a major contributor. One study compared two similar mergers where the major differentiator was the amount of communication taking place, and concluded that the increase in communication almost eliminated not only perceived uncertainty around the merger, but also typical negative effects of uncertainty such as stress and reduced productivity and retention.

However, since rumours cannot be quelled altogether, it is also important to feed in plenty of positive material – seek out opportunities for positive change (as discussed above) and make sure people are aware of them.

Finally, build credibility by ensuring you do not make promises which you cannot deliver.

Maintaining face-to-face communication

Face-to-face communication from top management can do a lot to alleviate uncertainty. While few companies take it as seriously as P&O/Stena, whose managers spent the day of the merger announcement in helicopters visiting fifteen locations to brief employees, most companies recognize face-to-face communication as an important element in the mix. The sooner top management are seen to be stating their position clearly, the sooner trust can be established and reliance on rumour reduced. It is also vital to act early to establish relationships between staff at all levels of both companies. One US company briefed employees of each company to visit and brief their counterparts in the other team. This did much to reassure employees about the company they were joining up with.

Face-to-face communication alone, however, frequently leaves gaps, whether due to managers' lack of communication skills or to the pressures of other tasks taking attention away from the need to talk to employees. In particular, many managers will be dealing with uncertainty about their own future, which is bound to have an impact on the success of the communication. Face-to-face briefing, then, is a vital tool, but should not be relied on to the exclusion of other methods.

Measure and learn

Communication for mergers and acquisitions can be one of the biggest learning experiences of a communicator's life. But if no plans are made to review the experience and capture the lessons learned, it will not happen.

Plan on measuring the impact of communication where it does occur, and the gaps where it does not. If possible, use a regular (weekly or monthly) survey to track progress, and learn from it as you go along. Check understanding of the key messages, and changes in attitude and behaviour.

Your measurement may show the positive aspects of the change, as well as the negative. When Hanson took over power generators, the Eastern Group, there was a widespread expectation that the acquiring company were asset-strippers who would destroy what the employees had worked so hard to build. In the event, the acquirers stuck with the existing management and business strategy, and demonstrated how much it valued the employees by enhancing the earnings of the staff share-save scheme. Ken Hunter, then Head of Communications at the Eastern Group, found that as a result of the takeover, 'Employee communications became a pleasure'.

Summary

The role that internal communicators can play in making a success of mergers and acquisition has long been undervalued.

However, a professional approach to planning and managing both pre- and post-acquisition communication can demonstrate substantial value-added.

References

Kernaghan, S., Clutterbuck, D. and Cage, S. (2001). *Transforming Internal Communication*. Business Intelligence.

Klasen, N. and Clutterbuck, D. (2002). *Implementing Mentoring Schemes – a Practical Guide to Successful Programs*. Butterworth-Heinemann.

Marks, L. and Mirvis, P. H. (2001). Making mergers and acquisitions work: strategic and psychological preparation. *Academy of Management Executive*, 15 (2), 80–94.

Vermeulen, F. and Barkema, H. G. (2001). Learning through Acquisitions. *Academy of Management Journal*, 44 (3), 457–476.

Building communication capability through interpersonal competence

The terms 'capability' and 'competence' are frequently confused, so it may be helpful to start this chapter with some definitions. Competence relates to a set of skills and knowledge, which an individual (or a team, or an organization) is able to apply to a practical task. The competencies movement, which has swept Human Resources in the past decade, is an attempt to define the basic skills required to operate at a specific level – for example, supervisor, middle manager or senior manager. Competencies frameworks often include items, such as 'exercising judgement', which are behavioural, as well as technical skills.

Competence is not the same as excellence, although it is often a precursor to excellence on the learning curve. To describe Pavarotti, Shakespeare or Jack Welch – to take examples from three different worlds – as merely competent is ludicrous. One useful way of looking at excellence, with regard to a specific competence, is that it represents a higher level of competence than that which is measured. One of the core discussions of the excellence movement in management in the 1980s was whether companies should set their targets on becoming and staying excellent. However, defining excellence was and is problematic, and many companies learned to their cost that it is necessary first to become competent, before you can aspire to excellence.

Competence exists independent of context and it is this that distinguishes it most clearly from capability, which is heavily dependent on context. Capability is the combination of competence with an environment in which the competence can be applied. At an individual level, for example, having the competence to make a magnificent presentation is of little value if there is no one ready and willing to listen. Similarly, the competence to inspire and motivate a team can be increased or decreased by the degree to which the organization permits and encourages informal dialogue during working hours or, if the team is scattered around the globe, by the difficulty of having real-time e-meetings that include all members at socially acceptable hours.

Contextual factors are many. They include the culture of the organization or industry, the nature of the markets, the technology available and language barriers.

Inevitably, this interaction between capability and competence has an impact on competence. The increasing use of e-communication means that managers in particular (but all employees in general) need to develop a whole set of skills around remote relationship-building. The better an individual, team or organization learns to understand and control its environment, the greater the demand to translate this learning into reproducible competencies.

Communication capability = communication competence + context

An additional distinction is that competence is based upon abilities already demonstrated, capability upon the *potential* to perform. When we say that someone has the potential to become a good manager, we are making a judgement based on the learning (i.e. competencies) they have demonstrated to date and on the attitudes they exhibit with regard to further development. The same is true with organizational capability. A stockbroker's analyst would assess a company on its potential to deliver improved results, with a large part of that assessment based upon past performance and future potential. Within future potential, the attitudes and behaviours of top management are key factors.

Communication capability is therefore in large part about the multitude of factors that make up potential. At an organizational level, key questions might include whether it can gain significant competitive advantage by communicating more effectively with its customers. At a team level, can the members interact more effectively so that the sum of their efforts significantly exceeds what would be achieved if they all worked in semi-isolation? At an individual level, what is the potential for me to influence people around me, to pursue the goals important to me? In all these cases, it is the exercise of capability that creates performance.

Performance = the exercise of capability

In this chapter, we will focus primarily upon competence, leaving other capability issues to Chapter 10. We have already identified three levels, at which competence can be expressed and measured: organization, team and individual. To these we can add a fourth and fifth – the employee communication function itself and the professionals within it. The links between these five levels are complex – as are the communication networks within the well-functioning organization (Figure 9.1).

The organization is an abstraction, which is partly represented by the top team. But organizations can function for quite a long time without leadership from the top. Organizational competence is something that permeates the entire structure. In essence, it is the result of the integration of all the levels of competencies,

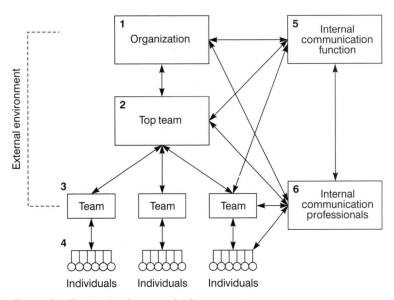

Figure 9.1 Five levels of communication competence

together with the organizational framework that makes that integration possible. Team communication competence is the ability of working units to manage communication between team members and between the team and other teams. Individual competence defines the skills people need to be able to manage interpersonal relationships in a way that ensures good communication and to make effective use of the information resources around them, be they IT, print or other people.

At the level of the internal communication function, competence relates to its ability to interface and integrate closely with the business priorities, providing the bridge between communication activity and the key business drivers. Finally, communication competence for the internal communication professional derives from the ability to work with people in the business to help them communicate more effectively. While this may sometimes involve doing some tasks for them (for example, planning a campaign or producing a periodical), the ownership of the communication issue should always rest with the internal client.

Let us look at these in more detail, starting with the organization.

Core competencies of the communicating organization

In Chapter 2, we explored in some depth how communication can be harnessed in support of organizational goals. However, we can also define a number of competencies that support these four pillars of organizational communication.

Organizational listening

The communication process starts with *listening*. Organizations that begin with the message miss the point. Whatever the audience, external or internal, understanding how receptive that audience is to different messages, and how to articulate its dreams as part of the organization's are essential precursors to designing messages that achieve their intended impact.

An organizational competence in listening will normally include:

- employing both formal and informal channels. Employee opinion surveys only provide answers to questions asked. Because surveys are designed by managers or consultants, not by the employees themselves, the issues most important to employees (and therefore most likely to affect the psychological contract) are often not covered. Using informal channels to listen is more likely to surface such concerns, which can be integrated into the formal surveys in due course. (It doesn't help that many organizations deliberately avoid surveying on issues, such as pay, on the grounds that doing so will stir up discontent.)

- listening constantly. Conducting major employee feedback exercises once a year, or even twice a year, is not an effective use of resources. It simply allows top management to tick the communication box and forget about it for a period. This is rather like relying on last year's annual report for deciding whether to buy shares in a quoted company. The annual report is merely a snapshot in time. As a predictor of what is happening in the company even a couple of months later it is of marginal value. Competence here requires a continuous programme of monitoring, at least monthly
- acknowledging what has been heard and demonstrating rational and timely responses to it
- encouraging everyone in the organization to listen actively to each, to key stakeholders, such as customers, and to share what they have learned.

Message clarity

Clarity of purpose demands a competence in getting the important messages straight, making them simple to articulate and emotive as well as intellectual. This is not simply a task for communication professionals; it is a partnership between them and the business leaders, with the primary responsibility resting with the latter.

Message consistency

Ensuring the consistency of messages over time demands active management. Consistency refers to more than saying the same thing, no matter who at senior level is delivering the message and no matter when. It also encompasses the ability to ensure that the words are supported by observable deeds and business decisions ('our future depends on our people' sounds hollow during a round of redundancies), and it encompasses consistency between different stakeholder audiences, a topic we covered in Chapter 4.

The ability to initiate and sustain dialogue

In most companies, listening and message-sending activities are separated at the organizational level. Gathering feedback from employees through questionnaires and focus groups does not engage them in an 'exchange of meaning'. Nor do the normal methods of disseminating messages, as we discussed briefly in Chapter 2. Creating the opportunities for reflection and exploration of issues with employees is vital in engaging their hearts and minds, for surfacing issues of concern to them, for gaining their understanding of the difficulty of some of the decisions that have to be made, for recognizing and making use of constructive consent, and for sustaining motivation.

Genuinely valuing diversity

Every organization develops a mindset and norms of behaviour that underpin its culture. This socialization process is remarkably swift. Within a few weeks, or at most months, people know what subjects to avoid, what kinds of opinion are respected and ignored, and what kind of behaviour will lead to approval or disapproval. In the 1980s, companies struggled hard to clone people into their cultural model, believing that this corporate cohesiveness was a strategic advantage, and many management gurus were quick to reassure them that this was the case. When these companies began to fail, it was at least in part because the corporate clones they had created were no longer a best fit with the environment in which the company operated. The stronger the culture, the greater the problems these companies have had in adapting to change, because the genetic mix of perspectives and personalities was not diverse enough to recognize and respond to change.

The ability to incorporate different views and approaches into the discussion of important issues for the business is now an essential competence.

When we get to discuss individual and team communication competencies, you will observe a number of parallels. Although the competencies at each level may be expressed differently and vary in context, there is a great deal of similarity between them.

Core competencies of the communicating team

Like the organization as a whole, the effective team requires clarity of purpose (translated into well-defined priorities), effective communication processes, good interpersonal relationships, and leadership that provides a sense of direction and a good role model for communication. Before we explore what that means in practice, let us be clear about what we mean by 'team'.

Teams differ from groups in a number of ways, the most common of which being that:

- they have a sense of shared purpose, usually based around a common task
- the members are relatively adaptable in the roles they play (i.e. there is some element of substitutability)
- they share information, understanding and expertise
- they support each other
- individuals accept personal discomfort or disadvantage for the greater good of the team as a whole.

Although companies often refer to groups of people, who work together – say on a particular project or in a department – as teams, the reality is that they are nothing of the sort. Only when the members interact in the ways we have just described, can they truly be called a team.

The confusion about the nature of teams does not stop there. In a major study of team learning ('Learning Teams', funded by the European Social Fund GB through the Hertfordshire Training and Enterprise Council) we identified at least six very different types of team commonly found in organizations (Table 9.1).

Stable teams

The most common type of team – and the immediate picture that most people have of a team – is the stable team. Here the same people work together on a similar task for long periods of time. Typical of the stable team would be the accounts function, an orchestra or a number of internal communication professionals working together in the same office. While there may be specializations in roles, each role is necessary to complete the task and each member needs to understand what the others are doing and why. Stable teams have the great benefit that people work with each other sufficiently often to develop this kind of understanding, to learn from each other and to build personal friendships – all of which aid communication.

At the same time, however, they can develop high levels of interpersonal conflict and stereotyping of people's roles. The conflict may appear either as open warfare or, more often, be buried by mutual consent, so that everyone either pretends not to notice dysfunctional behaviours or excuses them ('Oh, that's just Fred's way'). Or major problems with what the team does – say, with its customer service – are not brought up by the team member who observes them, because that might upset their colleague. The fact that the team has to get along together, at least superficially, means that communication often becomes super-ficial. One-off team-building events are more likely to exacerbate this situation than remedy it.

Table 9.1 Communication competence for different types of team

Stable teams	Surface and manage conflict Develop deep awareness of each other's motivations, skills and capabilities Learn from and with each other Induct new members effectively Absorb ideas and information from outside the team Stimulate creativity within the team Reflect frequently on the link between team activities and the team goals
Project team	Rapid creation of trust and mutual supportiveness Rapid agreement of clear goals, roles and priorities Sharing and building upon each other's ideas Maintaining a constant flow of information that keeps all the team members up to speed Keeping other stakeholders in the organization informed Skills to network and influence outside the team
Evolutionary teams	As project teams, plus: Explaining the evolution of the project and the thinking behind it
Cabin crew teams	Anticipating communication needs Providing fast, accurate and detailed information as soon as it is needed Being alert to visual as well as verbal and written clues Doing all of these under both normal conditions and under stress
Virtual teams (geographically separated)	Cultural sensitivity Remote relationship-building skills Anticipating communication needs Providing fast, accurate and detailed information as soon as it is needed
Virtual teams (networks plus)	Influencing skills The ability to develop and present a convincing business case The ability to acquire and cultivate champions
Development alliances	Understanding the other person's needs Drawing appropriately on memory and experience Conceptual modelling Storytelling Active listening Advanced questioning skills

Another significant communication problem with the stable team is that newcomers often find it very hard to fit in. People, who have worked together for a long time, develop their own vocabulary and meanings, shorthand references and norms of doing things that can seem impenetrable to the newcomer. In most cases, people have to pick up these nuances as best they can. Lacking the confidence that comes with full acceptance within the team, they frequently waste the opportunity of looking at the team's operation with fresh eyes and become sucked into the routine.

Paradoxically, the better people in the team get on together and the more tightly knit they are as a group, the greater the barriers to change. The more they learn to rely on each other, the less likely they are to look for ideas and innovation outside the team. Sometimes it is necessary to break up a reasonably well-functioning team, because it has become too cosy and insular.

Communication competencies for the stable team, therefore, include the ability to surface and manage conflict, to develop a deeper awareness of each other's motivations, skills and capabilities, to learn from each other, to induct new members in a way that contributes to team effectiveness and to maintain dialogue with a wide variety of external resources, to sustain constant renewal of ideas.

Project teams

Project teams are typically set up to deal with specific short-term issues – for example, introducing a new appraisal process, designing a new sales catalogue or communication around a specific event such as an acquisition. The membership is often drawn from other groups or teams, but is likely to be quite stable for the duration of the project. The task, however, is likely to be a new one for at least some of the team.

While project teams may be great environments for learning and for increasing personal visibility, they are often a communication nightmare. It takes time for the members to work through the stages of forming, storming and norming to performing. By the time they have got there – if they do – the team has been disbanded and the members have moved on. Communication competencies for project teams include: being able to speed up the creation of trust and mutual supportiveness; rapid agreement of clear goals, roles and priorities; sharing and building upon each other's ideas; and maintaining a constant flow of information that keeps all the team members up to speed, along, where appropriate, with other stakeholders in the organization.

Because they often have to operate across departmental boundaries, project teams also need the skills to network and influence through their members.

Evolutionary teams

Evolutionary teams are like project teams, but they tend to be much longer term and involve more people, typically in several waves. Here both the task and the team membership are constantly evolving. Setting up a new manufacturing location might involve a corporate strategic planning team to begin with. They would be joined by some senior managers, then by technical experts. As the planners drop out, construction people move in and so on until the plant opens its doors to the last wave, the employees who will work there. For the senior managers, who have been involved from the beginning, the process is relatively straightforward. They understand how things came about and why they have been done in particular ways. For someone who joined several waves later, the problem is like that for the new recruit joining the stable team, only much worse.

The principal competency required here – in addition to those needed by project teams – is the ability to bring each new recruit to the team up to speed very rapidly, not just with what has to be done but with how the thinking around the task evolved. Techniques, such as *retro-engineered learning*, which uses structured dialogue to unpack the thinking from the conception of the project to the thinking, can help overcome some of these communication issues. However, the whole panoply of media can be employed in different ways to address the problem.

Cabin crew teams

Cabin crew teams take their name from the aircraft industry, where the team of flight staff on a particular aircraft may come together only rarely, because of shift patterns. Although the team membership is very unstable, the task remains pretty much the same every trip. Other examples of this type of team include film crew or the crew that manage corporate events. In all these cases, they have to be able to get on with the job and people they do not know well instantly and instinctively. Unlike the project team, there is little need for communication for learning but a high need for communication to co-ordinate. Communication competencies include being able to anticipate communication needs, being able to provide fast, accurate and detailed information as soon as it is needed, being alert to visual as well as verbal and written clues, and being able to do all of these under normal conditions and under stress.

Virtual teams

These come in two forms. In one, virtuality is a function of separation, either by time or geography or both. There is little, if any, opportunity to bring the whole team together face to face, so relationship building is difficult. The potential for misunderstanding, duplication of work and cross-cultural conflict is immense, especially when it is also a project or evolutionary team. Yet this type of team is becoming more and more common in multinational organizations. Global teams are a rational response to global challenges.

Critical competencies for this type of virtual team include cultural sensitivity, remote relationship-building skills and the offline equivalent of the cabin crew's intuitive communication skills.

The second form of virtual team is unofficial, often invisible to anyone not a member. It can range from the 'skunk works' described by Peters and Waterman (1982) to communities of interest, such as all the compensation specialists in a multinational company. These loose groupings of people become a team when they agree to pool their knowledge, influence and creativity in pursuit of a common goal – usually to bring about a specific change in the organization. (A good example is an ethnic minority managers' network in a UK company. Over time, a smaller group came together, with the aim of making a radical change in recruitment and succession planning processes within the organization. As its influence began to be felt, it acquired first tacit then open support from top management, eventually being given substantial resources and evolving into a fully sanctioned project team.)

Critical communication competencies for this type of virtual team include influencing skills, the ability to develop and present a convincing business case and the ability to acquire and cultivate champions.

Development alliances

Finally, development alliances are a form of team which exists only or primarily for the sharing of experience and learning. Common examples might be an action learning set or a mentoring relationship between people at different levels in different functions. In these teams, the critical competencies for all the parties involved lie in understanding the other person's needs, drawing appropriately on memory and experience, conceptual modelling (being able to interpret issues and processes into diagrammatic form), storytelling, active listening and advanced questioning skills.

Over and above these genus-specific skills, all types of team require a number of generic communication competencies:

The ability to create and use effectively opportunities for reflective dialogue

Teams that communicate well between members all make time and space for stepping back and reviewing what they do and why – not just in a once or twice a year away-day, but frequently. Most team meetings are focused on specific problems and task priorities, but effective teams also take time out to look at the big picture and relate what they do to (a) the team goals and priorities, (b) benchmarks of good practice elsewhere and (c) ideals to which they would like to aspire. In doing so, they establish common understanding, common priorities and gain insights into each other's perspectives and contribution to the team.

An interest in the opinions and perspectives of other team members

Work pressure and work culture make it difficult in many organizations to see people beyond the role in which their work interacts with yours. This greatly limits the quality of the interactions we have with other people. Communicating teams are characterized in large part by the way that members listen and show respect to each other, valuing what they have to say even if it does not accord with their own views. In many ways, this is a prerequisite for reflective dialogue.

One of the benefits of such behaviour is that the quality of decisions is improved as less assertive members of the team offer differing views, or question assumptions the rest of the team has simply accepted at face value.

The ability to confront difficult issues in a positive and constructive manner

Daniel Goleman (1996) calls them 'lacunas' – the problems we conspire to ignore, because facing up to them is emotionally painful. Every team and every relationship is subject to them and for the most part, they provide the 'social lies' that enable us to operate cordially with other people. (How many husbands would dare to tell their wives that they look fat in that new dress? Or wives tell their husbands . . .) Eventually, however, lacunas can become so numerous or so serious that they have a negative effect on the morale and performance of the team. Knowing how to bring these issues into the open for discussion is an essential communication skill for members of senior level teams and desirable in all teams.

The ability to build and manage trust

With trust, confronting lacunas becomes a lot easier. The starting point is to accept that the other team members have a common interest with each other and goodwill towards each other. Without trust-building competence, effective communication is impossible at anything but a rudimentary level because every message is liable to be regarded with suspicion, or discounted, or both.

The ability to share learning and access learning from sources outside the team

In communicating teams, every member has a responsibility for gathering and sharing information, which may be useful to team colleagues. The learning teams study found that many effective teams encourage individuals to become knowledge specialists – to become the source of know-how and data about topics only they were substantially interested in, but which proved valuable to the team from time to time.

The ability to be inclusive

So many teams end up with an inner core and an outer ring of less well-informed employees. The ways, in which this happens, can be very subtle. For example, a manager who insists on holding important meetings after 5.00 p.m., when staff with childcare responsibilities cannot attend, is creating a two-tier information hierarchy. Shift-work, part-time work and other factors may make it difficult to be information inclusive, but communicating teams ensure they overcome these barriers.

Communication for the individual

Managers in the twenty-first century will differ from their twentieth-century counterparts in a number of ways, most of which can already be observed in some organizations. Many – indeed most – of these differences are essentially communication behaviours, as Table 9.2 illustrates. The items in Table 9.2 are relevant as generic communication competencies for managers. What they do not do is reflect the *situational* nature of communication in the workplace.

Table 9.2 The manager as communicator: twentieth-century versus twenty-first-century norms

Twentieth-century manager	Twenty-first-century manager
Manages by line of sight	Manages employees by outputs
Gives instructions	Explains goals and resources/restraints and encourages employees to work together to plan and complete the task
Spends more time telling than listening	Spends more time discussing and listening
Decides what employees need to know and when	Helps employees decide what they need to know and when
Calls meetings when manager feels it appropriate	Allows everyone to initiate meetings
Expected to have superior task knowledge	Recognizes that in a fast-moving field, the employees have the knowledge
Builds reputation on task competence and toughness	Builds reputation in addition on skills as a motivator and influencer
Work and personal lives are separate issues – employees should not let their personal lives interfere with work needs	Work and personal needs can and should be integrated – both are therefore legitimate areas for discussion between manager and employee
The big picture is not relevant to ordinary employees	Understanding the big picture is important in enabling people to be self-directing
Discourages criticism and open discussion	Constructive dissent and dialogue are essential to team cohesion
Training beyond the immediate task is a reward	Training for tomorrow's needs is a necessity
Is the link between the team and the 'outside' world (other departments, more senior levels)	Facilitates team members in building their own networks within and outside the organization
Interprets communication from above for the team	Discusses communication from above with the team to develop shared meaning
Largely ignores communication between team members	Encourages and facilitates communication between team members
Keeps own personal development plan to him or herself	Shares own development objectives with the team and asks for their help in achieving them
'Them and us' is part of the natural order	Builds trust across the manager/employee divide
Communication content mainly intellectual (task specific)	Communication content includes high level of relationship building
See time for reflection and team dialogue as lost production	See time for reflection and dialogue as essential in working smarter

Table 9.3 A situational matrix of communication

	One-to-one communication	One-to-group communication	One-to-many communication
Up to your managers	e.g. appraisal/ update	e.g. board presentation	e.g. addressing top management layers
Across to your peers	e.g. cross-functional project meeting	e.g. training session	e.g. sales conferences
Down to your direct reports	e.g. induction session	e.g. team briefing	e.g. roadshow

Some years ago, **item** investigated, on behalf of a group of client companies, why managers so often disagreed with how they were appraised as communicators. Was it because they did not want to admit how bad they were, or were there more subtle factors at work? Two factors emerged from the focus group interviews. One was that communication is a two-way activity and so the appraiser often contributed heavily to the communication failure. The second was that appraising a manager on his or her presenting ability, for example, provided only a very partial picture, especially if making presentations was not an important part of their job.

With the help of Birkbeck College, London, a *situational map* of communication emerged (see Table 9.3). All communication situations at work fell into one of the nine boxes of the map, defined by the size of the audience and the power distance[1] felt by the person communicating. So giving instruction and giving a performance appraisal would fall in the same box. In another, non-work context, the same supervisor and employee might feel themselves to be peer to peer, or the roles may be reversed.

Within the nine situational boxes, the same communication skills occur, in a clear cycle, as shown in Figure 9.2. Effective dialogue consists in each case of opening (starting the conversation), transmitting (getting the message across), receiving/

[1] Power distance describes the level of comfort/discomfort a person feels with someone else. There may be a high power distance between a young graduate recruit and a senior manager, for example, although both may gradually overcome this feeling. Power distance is much greater in some cultures (Indonesia, France) than others (UK, Scandinavia). For the purposes of this study power distance is loosely defined as whether the relationship is superior to inferior, inferior to superior, or peer to peer.

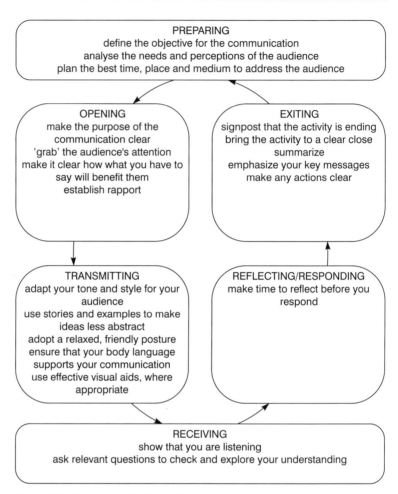

Figure 9.2 The communication cycle

sensing (listening to and observing a response), reflecting (thinking about what you have heard), responding (formulating an answer) and exiting (finishing the conversation, or part of it). In practice, people often carry out some of these elements in parallel. Whether it is appropriate to do so depends on the situation: receiving reflecting and responding at the same time may be useful in the context of a brainstorm, but less helpful in a complex negotiation.

In addition, each situation calls for subtly different interpretations of each element and of communication style. Listening to someone else giving a speech is different to listening to an audience when you are the speaker, and different again from listening to a direct report and to listening to someone to whom you are giving an appraisal. These subtle nuances are learned as a child, but very few people learn them perfectly. Raising awareness of each situation and how we manage each element of the communication cycle is the first, critical, step in improving an individual's overall communication competence.

item has found that focusing on those specific situations, where the individual needs to communicate well and where feedback from the other parties in the communication exchange indicates a need for improvement, is a pragmatic approach to competence development. In particular, when the individual has an opportunity to practise the specific skills in similar, simulated situations in the unthreatening environment of a development workshop, radical improvements occur. Even more so,when they are able subsequently to gather feedback in the real workplace, in those situations.

This approach also often helps identify those who have become stereotyped as good communicators, but are really simply good talkers. Many professionals, who one would expect to be good all-round communicators, are far from it. Good journalists are often more adept at listening than talking (bad ones tend to be the opposite) and many politicians appear to have no listening skills at all.

Using a communication style appropriate to the situation is also an element of communication competence. But what exactly is communication style? For years, we used a diagnostic from the USA, based on four of the eight elements of the Myers-Briggs personality-type indicator. Problems applying it in real-life failures of communication between people led us to review the assumptions behind this kind of test. From focus groups with managers, it soon became clear that the central hypothesis of this and similar diagnostics – that communication style was simply a reflection of personality traits – was fundamentally flawed. Although personality is one of the influencing factors on communication style, it is but one. Equally important are factors such as the speed of communicating, the purpose of the exchange and the role the individual is required to play in that exchange. Being a good communicator is not a matter of having one style or another, but of being able to adapt style appropriately to the contextual requirements (purpose and role) of the situation and the ability of the other party(ies) to show similar style flexibility.

The four style dimensions that emerge from this analysis are expanding versus focusing; the tortoise versus the hare; logic versus empathy; and influencing versus conciliating.

Expander versus focuser

Expanders tend to be intuitive thinkers, fascinated by ideas and things new. They often have great difficulty keeping to the subject, because they constantly see new possibilities. They can be very good at extrapolating from relatively thin data, sometimes making leaps of logic that only they can follow – but may often be broadly correct. They can often appear to other people as rambling and incoherent. Their favourite phrases include 'Yes . . . and . . .' and 'Here's another way of looking at the issue . . .'.

Focusers like to concentrate on one thing at a time and deal with it thoroughly. The vaguer a concept is, the more they feel the need to narrow the discussion, until there is something they can pin down. They are not necessarily without creativity but they do not tolerate well uncertainty and ambiguity. They need to have a clear agenda for the discussion or dialogue. Their favourite phrases include 'Let's be clear what we mean', 'Let's get back to the point' and 'What are we trying to achieve here?'

Tortoise versus hare

Tortoises like to think before they speak. This may be partly from concern not to embarrass themselves, but it is primarily a matter of needing to assess and weigh as they go along. They need to be sure they have understood each step of an argument before they proceed to the next. Tortoises often leave much unsaid. Depending on circumstance, they can be seen at the extremes as 'deep thinkers' or as dullards. They may switch out of a discussion for a while to ponder a statement or concept, then switch back when things have moved on. Their favourite phrases include: 'Can we just stop and think about where we're going with this?' and 'Can we just back up a bit?'

Hares talk fast and a lot. They may often be perceived by tortoises as shallow, as overly concerned with presentation at the expense of content. They often see the implications of an argument long ahead of other people and may make their mind up about what to do before they have listened fully to the arguments. They may be seen most positively as decisive and productive, but others may see them as impetuous. Their favourite phrases include, 'We have too many meetings here' and 'This is getting too detailed'.

Logician versus empath

Logicians are determined to ensure that discussions are intellectually sound. They like to see the framework of a concept and test it against their perception of reality and coherence. They can be seen at their best as rigorous; at worst, as cold, pedantic and argumentative. They accept no statement at face value and they may appear to others to pursue insignificant details to distraction, because something does not fit their pattern of logic. They are more concerned with being right than with building concensus. Their favourite phrases may include, 'Where's the proof?' or 'I don't think this hangs together'.

Empaths are very good at sensing other people's feelings. They like to establish good rapport before they start a discussion and they are keen to understand other people's viewpoints. They can be adept at concensus-building and ensuring others are included in discussions. Their very sensitivity may, however, make them 'prickly'. They evaluate ideas and arguments less by their logic than by how they feel about them, or expect others to feel about them. Their favourite phrases may include: 'I'm not happy about this' or 'How will other people react to this?'

Influencer versus conciliator

Influencers like to get their own way. They are clear about their objectives for communicating and sometimes aggressive in achieving them. They employ consensus-building only as long as it leads towards the answer they intended. They expend a lot of energy trying to bring others around to their viewpoint. They may be seen positively as visionary and results orientated; negatively as obsessive, confrontational and egotistical. Their favourite phrases include, 'I can't see your problem' or 'We (meaning I) need to make a decision'.

Conciliators are concerned with keeping the group together and united. They are less worried about the outcomes of a discussion than the process by which decisions are reached. They are prepared to subordinate their own views to those of the group, or to the other person in a one-to-one discussion, if that will ensure a broadly acceptable outcome. They will always prefer negotiation to confrontation. From a negative perspective, they may appear weak and unassertive; from the positive, they help to ensure that decisions taken have a broad commitment necessary from all parties if those decisions are to be imple- mented effectively. Their favourite phrases include, 'We're all in the same boat' and 'Let's not over-react . . .'.

Individual competence in communication is therefore much more complex than it is usually portrayed.

Competencies of the internal communication function

The initial research for our study of the link between business performance and the performance of the communication func- tion involved a massive literature search and a mixture of one-to- one a focus group interviews with experienced professionals (see Chapter 2). It also extracted views from CEOs and other key internal clients.

The net result – the four critical communication competencies as defined by these various sources – was the basis of our initial comparisons:

- Having a *communication strategy*. (Although the experts and practitioners generally agreed this should be linked to business priorities, there was little agreement about how to do so.)
- Effective *management processes* to implement the plan.
- Experienced and capable *communication professionals*.
- High-quality *communication media and tools*.

None of these competencies showed a *direct* link with business performance. However, they do appear to have an indirect link, expressed when they are used in support of the four strategic pillars of communication.

One thing stands out about all these competencies. They are about what the function and its professionals do directly, rather than how they enable others to communicate effectively. We now therefore add a fifth functional competence: *influencing communication capability within the organization*. This may be expressed in many ways. For example, selling top management on the value of paying more attention to their own communication, promoting better practice in communication between individuals and/or other departments, or encouraging networking and open dialogue.

Part of the value of our research project was that it emphasized the difference between performance (how the efforts of a communication function should be evaluated by the business) and competence (the underlying skills that enable it to deliver desired results). What has happened in many organizations – and not just with regard to the internal communication function – is that the two have become confused. To assess performance properly, it is necessary to ask: 'What has this function done to contribute to the achievement of business goals and priorities?' To assess competence, the question is: 'To what extent does it have the skills to do the job?' Having the skills and applying them appropriately are not the same thing. But without the skills, it is much more difficult to achieve the performance required.

Core competencies for the internal communication professional

As employee communication becomes an essential and recognized business discipline, expectations of those who work in this relatively new profession are increasing rapidly. Having some journalistic or public relations skills is not enough. Being able to write well is merely a starting point. At a senior level, the new professionals require:

- a working knowledge of marketing, human resources, finance, logistics and information technology (as a minimum)
- the ability to understand and translate strategy, at both the conceptual and practical levels
- the ability to integrate media, to develop and implement effective communication plans, and to manage complex projects
- the ability to link communication activities firmly to business priorities
- an appreciation of the cultural dimension of employee communication and an ability to take cultural and diversity issues into account in communication activities
- practical knowledge and experience of managing the communication of major change initiatives – for example, merger and acquisition, branding, downsizing, major technological change
- the ability to carry out effective benchmarking with other organizations
- the ability to measure the effectiveness of communication; and to measure
- effective service quality management skills
- the ability to be a role model for communication competencies, including networking, presenting and listening skills and written communication in a wide range of media
- the ability to collaborate with Human Resources/training in designing and implementing programmes to improve the communication capability of managers and others in the organization
- the ability and motivation to coach others in communication skills
- general skills of internal consultancy.

This is quite a catalogue and it is evident that relatively few of the competencies suggested here are *communication skills* per se. The essence of the role is to combine knowledge of good communication practice with good management. To partner with senior managers, the internal communication specialist must develop a high degree of empathy with the mix of strategic and tactical thinking that characterizes decision-making at the top. Indeed, some organizations, such as Government Information and Communication Services (GICS) have taken the view that, for appraisal purposes at least, internal communication managers should be evaluated on exactly the same competence checklist as any other manager.

Of course, at a more junior level within the function, there will continue to be many roles for specialists, just as there are in Human Resources and other disciplines. Each of the thirteen competencies described above can be scaled down, however, to be appropriate to these individuals. If they want to become a real professional, however, they will need to develop a high level of each competence. To do so, they may well have to spend some time outside the internal communication function, in positions that offer more hands-on managerial experience.

One of the positive factors in this picture is that people come into internal communication from a wide variety of other disciplines and often bring line management experience (and therefore credibility) with them. A very few arrive with extensive experience in strategic planning, but this is a route which should grow in popularity as the link between communication activity and the achievement of business strategy achieves greater acceptance.

Summary: a holistic view of communication competence

What we hope this chapter has achieved as a minimum is to raise serious questions about the simplistic way, in which communication competence within organizations has traditionally been regarded. Whether it be at organization, team or individual level, the contextual situational nature of effective communication demands a much deeper understanding of the complexities of good communication, and the development of instinctive appropriate responses to different situations. At an organizational level, for example, digging out the M&A manual (while better than having no planned response at all) is a less effective response to a communication need than having a cadre of both communication specialists and ordinary managers across the organization who know exactly what to do, having experienced the situation before, either for real or in simulation.

In general, the situation in most organizations with regard to communication competencies can be summarized as follows:

- Communication competence is only defined and measured in one or two of the five areas we have explored, if that many.
- Where individual communication competence is appraised, it is based on inadequate models of communication – a

Cinderella topic in much broader frameworks of leadership competence generated by or for Human Resources, with little or no input from communication professionals.

- There is little or no attempt at an integrated approach to communication competence at organization, team and individual levels. Only just over half of British companies have a planned process for improving communication competence in the organization (according to the study *Transforming Internal Communication*; Kernaghan, Clutterbuck and Cage, 2001). Nor is there often an attempt to integrate the activities of the communication function and the professionals within it, with development of communication competence.

If top management of companies truly believes that communication is a strategic competence, one which will have the potential to establish real and sustainable competitive advantage, it will increasingly demand answers to questions such as:

- Where do we have to establish and maintain a high level of communication competence in this business?
- How will we define what communication competence is, in each of those contexts?
- How will we measure the degree and quality of that competence?
- What targets should we set?
- What resources will be needed to raise the level of communication competence wherever it is needed?
- What are our priorities in building communication competence?
- Whose responsibility is it? (Top management's? The communication function's? Human Resources'? Line managers'? Some internal consortium?)

This chapter should have given a lot of helpful starting points, but the sheer lack of significant work in this whole area means that there is a lot of work to do in even planning a coherent response to these questions. Elsewhere in the book, we explore the issue of reputation of the internal communication function. One of the best ways we can suggest of raising that reputation with top management is to be the first to pose these questions and to enter into a partnership with top management to establish pragmatic answers. In many, perhaps most organizations, the door will already be at least partially open. No CEO wants his or her organization to underperform in communication terms. The fact that these issues do not have high priority is simply a reflection of the lack of a credible, business-performance led method of approaching them. The heroes of this century's businesses will increasingly be those functional managers who not only identify an issue for the business, but quantify it and propose realistic approaches for major improvement. In other words, the IC professional must move from a strategically reactive stance to a strategically proactive one.

References

Goleman, D. (1996). *Vital Lies Simple Truths: The Psychology of Self-Deception*. Touchstone.

Kernaghan, S., Clutterbuck, D. and Cage, S. (2001). *Transforming Internal Communication*. Business Intelligence.

Peters, T. J. and Waterman, R. H. (1982). *In Search of Excellence*. Harper and Row.

Building communication capability through technology

While the dot.com explosion provided audiences with a dazzling spectacle, an equivalent – but much quieter – revolution was taking place inside medium-sized and large organizations. And where dot.com businesses typically proved to be a fireworks display, all bang and brilliant lights but of little impact, internal e-communication may yet prove the opposite; quiet and stealthy, but intensely effective.

For certain, the value of internal e-communication as a means of providing widespread access to shared resources is undeniable. The company directory, policies and procedures, design templates, a real-time share price, breaking news, flexible benefits; these and many other online resources have already provided real and measurable benefits, not least in terms of the money saved on producing and distributing equivalent print versions of these reference materials.

But the vision that coaxed the boardroom into opening its chequebook was sexier than simply offering access to shared resources. It was one of a new competitive landscape where the underpinning infrastructure would create a global organization that could 'electrify' itself to electrify its customers through outstanding service; one in which different markets would resolve common problems by pooling their knowledge and experience.

The age of instant internal broadcast would also have a profound and beneficial impact on the morale and shared purpose of the organization, where the glue that bonded people to each other and their company grew ever more cohesive.

Yet while there are some outstanding examples of success, there are perhaps fewer than are claimed. The truth is that it takes substantial and sustained effort to stimulate employees into making full use of the tools available to them to share knowledge and keep it fresh.

And as can happen in large organizations, the people who make the promise are not the ones who have to deliver it. The vision was most frequently painted by IT; but now, as often as not, the board is looking to its communicators to make it come true.

The communicating organization

One of the hard truths of the intranet age is the investment in hardware and software has more often increased the quantity of communication than its effectiveness at engaging and motivating.

The reason? Much of that investment has been made on the premise that 'if you build it, they will come'. Yet, as we saw in Chapter 1, channels that are effective at distributing information – however well thought out and presented – are not necessarily an effective way to engage audiences. Even the CEO's live intranet broadcasts soon lose their power, as audiences grow accustomed to the technology and recognize that being able to see is not the same as being able to participate or engage in dialogue.

E-fatigue (for want of a better expression) has been exacerbated by the way intranets are constructed. All energy focuses on the launch date, on building intranets and filling them with content. Yet too often they stay unchanged over the following eighteen months before the next release. Where they do change, content quality is questionable and look and feel begins to diverge from the template – and communicators, who simply do not have the time or energy to act as intranet police (after all, that is what the content management system is for) fall into despair.

So what can communicators do? Many communicators come from a traditional background; comfortable with print, less so with e-media. They do not know the technical vocabulary sufficiently to participate in discussions with information technologists, and so take advice on faith. But communicators have a greater responsibility than that: they owe it to their organizations to understand and get involved. If nothing else, they can contribute their experience and understanding of human nature. The intranet is a tool, after all; the technology exists not for its own sake, but to enable communication, access to resources and interaction.

For example, technologists often approach the challenge of e-communications by contemplating what technology *can* achieve, not what the organization (and its employees) need.

Communicators intuitively understand that providing value through an intranet demands certain attributes: navigation and content should be designed for the benefit of users, not contributors; it should resolve questions swiftly and provide accurate, up-to-date resources; it must be intuitive, well written and laid out; all content reflects on the credibility of all other content, so it all needs to maintain the same standards; it should be dynamic and, occasionally, startling.

It also needs to be measurable.

Auditing success

As the focus shifts from cost saving to building competitive advantage, boardrooms are increasingly demanding evidence of value to justify investment. Yet providing compelling evidence is not easy. Analysing intranet statistics is complex and not particularly illuminating. While user logs can guide on trends, they are less helpful at explaining underlying reasons – or the intentions, recollection or reactions of the audience. It does not capture knowledge sharing, motivation and behaviour change. It does not mirror the impact on business performance or on achieving strategic objectives.

So what should you do? First, get a clear idea of your purpose. Corporate intranets often came into being following a command from the CEO, and were put together by 'Babel Tower' teams from HR, IT and communications – each with different skills, ambitions, understanding and hopes. It is often a salutary exercise to remind yourself exactly what your organization expects from its e-media, whether it is saving print costs, strengthening the 'corporate glue', enhancing branding, broadcasting company news, mechanizing business intelligence and knowledge management, encouraging a forum for knowledge and best practice sharing or enhancing the sense of community. To any organization or CEO answering all of the above, the reply is 'no way'.

Ask yourself how realistic your ambitions are, and then begin to consider where you currently stand against them. Survey users to find out what proportion of them use the intranet, why, whether they enjoy the experience and trust the information published? Ask what frustrates them, and where they most often break down. Learn how e-communication fits with print and face to face in the current communication mix – and what they would like it to be. And don't make the mistake of only providing the questionnaire on the Intranet – the views of non-users may be as valuable as those of users, if not more so.

Armed with this information, you will have a much stronger case to make, both with the board and with colleagues from IT.

The four pillars

One key tool in evaluating new communication technology is assessing what contribution it makes to each of the four pillars.

Clarity of purpose

Clarity of purpose is not helped by excessive noise in the system. While trying to *control* communication from other parts of the business may not be practical, internal communication can help by:

- providing advice to help managers link what they want to say more clearly to business priorities and values
- creating media that managers *want* to use to communicate to the organization, and which frame messages and feedback in ways that support the business purpose
- measuring the effectiveness of all internal media, whether under the control of the function or not, against how they support the business purpose
- helping the organization focus on quality rather than quantity of communication, so that the important messages stand out, both from and to the centre. This might mean, for example, educating people on how to target and structure electronic communication.

Top management behaviour

Helping top management consider and manage the balance of how they communicate – and the impact of their behaviour – is an essential role for the senior internal communicator.

The impact of new technologies on top management communication behaviour has been both positive and negative. On the positive side, there are far more ways in which they can reach and be reached by internal audiences and these tend to be more immediate. There is also greater possibility to engage in timely dialogue with internal stakeholders on issues that affect them.

On the other hand, it is very easy for top management to become overdependent on remote media, at the expense of spending time discussing face to face, or walking the talk where employees work.

Effective information sharing

In theory, the new technologies have been a boon to information sharing. But quantity is no substitute for quality. In most organizations people find that there is too much information in general and not enough that is truly relevant, useful and timely. The key to effective systems for sharing information and know-how is that they involve a judicious and balanced mixture of processes, both electronic and face to face, and access to both explicit information, which is normally structured and stored, and tacit information, which is highly context specific.

People's need for information depends very much on circumstance. While simple instructions on how to complete an application form for a training programme can easily be stored on a web site, advice on how a line manager should go about firing an employee for misconduct would typically require a one-to-one discussion with an expert.

One company that has worked hard to establish an appropriate balance between the different ways of sharing information is the computer services company Xansa. It has placed most of the routine personnel administration data on its intranet but still maintains an HR call centre, staffed by members of the HR team in rotation, to which managers can address the enquiries that require a more considered response.

Trusting interfaces

While electronic communication can earn *credibility* (for the reliability, freshness and accuracy of their content) it is harder to replace the empathetic bond of *trust* that can exist between close-knit teams, and between managers and their reports.

Being able to distinguish between the kind of information that can be shared electronically and that which benefits from personal interface is therefore a key skill for communicators.

Sharing explicit information typically involves providing people with routinized processes and standard knowledge. It requires little or no discussion and can usually be managed through from reports, handbooks, web sites or other forms of information capture. On the rare occasions it does require discussion, this tends to be around supplying missing detail.

Sharing tacit information almost always requires dialogue. While face to face is normally most effective, electronic sharing can also be very useful if both parties are prepared to be open and reflective. The problems occur when people try to use one-way media, such as a passive web site, when the information the user requires is intuitive, subjective or demands complex judgement – or when people waste time holding meetings about information that would have been much better circulated as a memorandum.

Where are we going?

The emergence of communications technology within organizations is posing subtler – but perhaps more far-reaching – questions about the nature of the psychological contract between employees and their organizations

For example, now that we can reach all employees, all the time, wherever they are, what do we do with that capability? Anyone who has been woken at 4 a.m. or dragged from their holiday poolside to participate in a conference call, recognizes that connecting technology can be a curse as well as a blessing.

e-Mails do not stop because you are at home or on holiday. Our whereabouts can be constantly known – our cars tagged for congestion charging, our strolls monitored for security. As our mobile phones are becoming mobile computers and businesses operate on international time, so the line between work and non-work time becomes increasingly blurred.

One critical response is likely to be an intense desire by people to find privacy and protection from intrusion in other ways. The use of artificial intelligence (AI) to screen out all unwanted messages is a near certainty.

This poses its own set of challenges for communicators. Instead of forcing information upon people, the secret is to make audiences want to access it, either on their own initiative or at the instigation of their AI gateway, which knows the kind of choices and interests they will have. Internal communicators are already aware of the difficulty of persuading people to pay attention to messages from the centre or from staff functions; they will need to develop new approaches to convince people to 'tune in'.

Twenty-four hour availability will have some business advantages. It will allow urgent issues to be discussed and dealt with as they occur, no matter where the decision-makers are. But there will be a price to pay in the continued blurring of work and non-work lives. The implications of this for the psychological contract between the organization and its employees are vast.

Learning to live and work in an instant information society will not be easy. Many people have not adapted to the relatively minor changes already wrought by the Internet and the mobile phone. To make full use of the opportunities presented by tomorrow's technologies, the internal communication function should be working now with the HR and training functions to plan training interventions that will help people do far more than cope.

An associated issue is that of privacy. Questions are already being raised about how individuals or companies can retain any semblance of privacy in an environment where personal and corporate details are so widely spread and hard to protect – a world that is so dependent on such a small number of designs of operating systems is increasingly open to legal and illegal intrusion.

Information transparency is the new reality. So how can companies cope? One answer is simply to learn to live with openness. The less information you need to keep secret, the less of a problem you have. In an information society, businesses can gain competitive advantage less by holding back knowledge than by:

- sharing it as widely as possible, with collaborators who will reciprocate
- encouraging employees to build and exploit extensive networks of open information exchange – including with competitors
- becoming more efficient at collating, analysing and making use of information.

Applications overload

It is a truism to say that deriving value from electronic applications depends on users making the most of them. Yet, rather than use new technologies to their full capability, many people adapt to their use in a small range of activities where it is useful or there is no practical alternative. In effect, they make a cost-benefit calculation, where the cost involves both the effort to learn new tricks and often an innate fear of new technology, while the benefit is the perceived utility of the new skill.

The trick, then, is to provide enabling technology *that people will use*. As yet, few employers actively engage employees in debate about which technologies to invest in and why. Where such decisions relate to how products affect the outside world, they are seen as the province of the marketers and strategic planners; where they relate to internal processes – for example, how products are made – they are seen as the province of operations and/or research and development.

However, employees, like the populace in general, are giving less and less credence to experts. Enabling employees to question the experts, to voice their concerns and to become part-owners of the decisions will build commitment to the business and its strategies. Opening up the dialogue to other stakeholders is also likely to have substantial benefits.

While technology brings advantages and new disciplines, it often has a temporary accompanying 'deskilling' effect – and can therefore cause anxiety among those potentially affected. Understanding how technology narrows and expands skills is essential in maintaining a relatively high level of job satisfaction. By and large, however, companies have little idea where they are in this cycle.

Well-designed feedback methods can provide organizations with the data they need to manage fears as well as enabling them to think creatively about the design of jobs to sustain people's sense of challenge and worth. The benefits should be seen in higher motivation, retention and commitment to change.

CHAPTER 11

Consolidating communication capability

The concept of the 'communicating company' is one, which has absorbed a great deal of our interest in recent years. We have had two main concerns: defining the 'communicating company' and establishing what precisely today's companies need to do to acquire that sobriquet.

This chapter also aims to consolidate the key lessons in this book, putting them into the broader contexts of *what do we need to do to enable the employee communication to fulfil its potential within the organization* and *what does the organization need to do to harness the power of communication, in achieving its goals?*

Let us start with some reality checks. As we have seen from Chapter 1 onwards, the IC function is not going to have a great deal of impact – no matter how professional its staff may be – unless it focuses its activities and resources on areas that will make a genuine difference to the business. A radical shift from an input orientation to an outcomes orientation is a critical first step. Having the active support of the business leaders – both intellectually and emotionally, in action as well as in word – is also essential. Without these basic foundations stones, the communication edifice will always be built on sand.

At the same time, it has to be recognized that effective communication is no panacea. It will not safeguard the business from unexpected market meltdown, as in the wake of the events of 11 September 2001. It will not protect it from the effects of bad management decisions such as a confusing name change, or a major hit to corporate reputation as occurred to international auditors Andersen as a result of the collapse of energy giant Enron. It does, however, have the power to reduce the likelihood and/or impact of such events. Open communication within a company is far more likely to identify malpractice than secrecy; calls to rally round and cope with misfortune work better when they fall on the ears of people, who are already motivated to trust their employer. Customers are more likely to remain with a provider which has invested in building trust, even if that trust is broken – as long as it communicates openly and honestly with them about its mistakes.

Taking the negative perspective, while being a communicating company will not necessarily guarantee business success, our research shows that poor communication will almost certainly make success harder to achieve.

So what is a 'communicating company' and how would you recognize one if you saw it? Some of the characteristics we would expect to find are:

- a high level of clarity about the role of communication in achieving business goals
- the long-range business plan contains a commensurately detailed communication plan
- clarity at the individual level about each person's responsibilities in making communication happen
- integration of communication policy and process across all functions and activities of the business
- support for individuals and functions in raising their communication competence is readily available, well targeted and highly effective
- role models for communication effectiveness are to be found widely throughout the organization (not just among the leadership)
- positive dialogue predominates over debate and/or argument; listening over broadcasting
- barriers to communication are rapidly identified and removed
- ideas percolate rapidly through the organization
- what the business says about itself is recognized as broadly true by both internal and external audiences
- there is no confusion – internally or externally – between the four expressions of brand
- the culture of the organization is such that people are truly able to express what they think and feel, without fear or discomfort

- informal networks and the grapevine usually support the business goals rather than undermine them
- there are no restrictions on who can talk to whom; everyone is available to everyone else, no matter where they sit in the hierarchy or which department or subsidiary they work in
- a wide range of technologies and media is used to communicate; each is regularly reviewed for its contribution to business goals
- people have the skills and self-discipline not to misuse media (e.g. e-mailing over-widely to protect one's back)
- feedback systems that both gather data constantly and require considered responses
- people in the field feel a valued part of the communication 'family'
- communication resource is concentrated at the point, where identity lies
- consideration of the communication issues is built into the early stages of all planning activities, from the business plan, through acquisitions, to relatively minor change initiatives
- stakeholders communication is both actively managed and integrated; the company effectively becomes an enabler for dialogue between communities – a dialogue which it can then both influence and learn from
- employee communication budgets are set not against the cost of continuing media, but in relation to the contribution the function is required to make towards specific business objectives

This quite lengthy list is far from exhaustive. It also mixes issues that range from the deeply philosophical to the immediately practical – yet each represents a common problem the modern organization faces every day. So perhaps the simplest way of defining the 'communicating company', is that it *recognizes, takes responsibility for and is determined to achieve excellence in all aspects of communication that contribute to the successful achievement of business goals*. In many or most cases, that contribution will be indirect rather than direct, yet it is still vital and measurable.

How should employee communication fit into the business structure?

Note that we did not entitle this section 'Who should employee communication report to?' If communication within the top team is working well, the reporting line to the top is of less importance

Table 11.1 Where does internal communication belong?

	For	*Against*
Public affairs	They are both communication disciplines	Internal communication is not about selling
	Integration of message between internal and external is important	Internal communication should have a higher emphasis on listening
Human Resources	HR has a stronger understanding of employee issues	HR people typically lack the journalistic skills
	HR 'owns' the learning dimension of communication	HR is not always trusted by employees
CEO's office	The CEO is or should be the champion of employee communication	Too many direct reporting lines reduce the CEO's efficiency

than the strength and scope of its remit in making communication work to the benefit of the business.

Our surveys of internal communicators and business leaders provide a very mixed picture as to perceptions of the benefits of attaching internal communication to Human Resources, Public Affairs, or direct to the Chief Executive's office. A brief summary of the arguments for and against is contained in Table 11.1.

In our view, this simply emphasizes the need to establish structures that ensure IC is not regarded as a discrete activity to be filed in one departmental chart or another, but as a cross-business discipline that can only operate effectively if it is incorporated into *all* the business processes. A 'communicating company', then, will have progressed the debate from *where does internal commmunication sit?* to *how do we integrate it into the business fabric?*

Stages of becoming a communicating company

The journey towards communicating company status is likely to be a fairly long and difficult one. It requires a substantial change of attitudes at all levels and a considerable investment in training and infrastructure. We have identified four broad stages of development towards becoming a communicating company:

1 *Nascent*. Communicates when it has to. Lots of commercial secrecy. Communication competence is largely haphazard. What development there is in communication skills is mostly crisis intervention.
2 *Immature*. Lots of discrete communication activities. Communication competence development confined mainly to leaders.
3 *Adolescent*. Integrated communication activities, mainly within functional silos. Communication competence development seen as an issue for customer-facing people as well as leaders.
4 *Adult*. Fully integrated across functions. Communication competence development seen as an issue for *all* employees.

How do you become a communicating company?

Planning to become a communicating company requires a collaborative effort from across the organization. As with any major change, it is important to:

1 Recognize where you are now.
2 Define where you want to be.
3 Evolve the plan to bridge the gap.

Recognizing where you are now demands a rigorous analysis of how communication works in the organization.

- How consistent are the messages people receive from different functions and departments?
- How competent are people at each level in communicating, and in sharing understanding, feelings and knowledge?
- How close to seamless is the communication chain between backroom employees and customers/other external stakeholders, and between top management and people at the lower levels?
- How much 'reinventing of the wheel' takes place?
- To what extent do people trust their colleagues in other departments or at other levels?
- Are there sufficient role models of effective communication?
- Does the technology make for better communication or get in the way?
- Do informal networks operate for or against the benefit of the organization?

Most of these questions will elicit a mixture of positive and negative answers – a patchwork quilt of communication performance. Nonetheless, these responses are the building bricks, with which a communication development plan can be built. In our experience, very few companies, if any, are able to do more than make a best guess on the answers to these questions.

Defining where you want to be requires some clarity about who *you* are. Of course, the people in the communication function have some ambitions, both personally and for the function, based on their own interests and ambitions. As the IABC research has shown, however, these may not be aligned closely with what the *organization* wants. Establishing organizational need again requires detailed research and analysis, but some basic starting questions include:

- How could improvements in communication facilitate the achievement of competitive differentiation, and medium and long-term business goals?
- What degree of influence could the communication function exert in helping change people's beliefs and behaviours to be closer in line with the corporate brand and the espoused values?
- How much more could the communication function do in supporting other functions in implementing their strategies?
- What core skills will a world-class communication function demonstrate in five years' time?

Initiating this kind of dialogue produces a radically different view of where the emphasis of the communication function's resource allocation and mental effort should lie. For example, one issue that comes to the fore in such discussion is the role of networking and virtual teams. Until now, companies have generally taken a fairly relaxed and benevolent view of these unofficial exchanges of information and influence (although occasionally trying to exert some control over the grapevine when its conjectures get too close to the truth for comfort). In future, however, organizations will need to encourage informal networks and virtual teams, because formal structures will be too slow for many key decisions. A role is therefore emerging, somewhere between internal communication and HR, for encouraging and supporting more effective networking, through new technology, training, role modelling and team learning.

Communications as a process is likely in the future to require all the communicating departments to surrender some of their independence in return for greater effectiveness. The kind of structure that may evolve is represented in Figure 11.1.

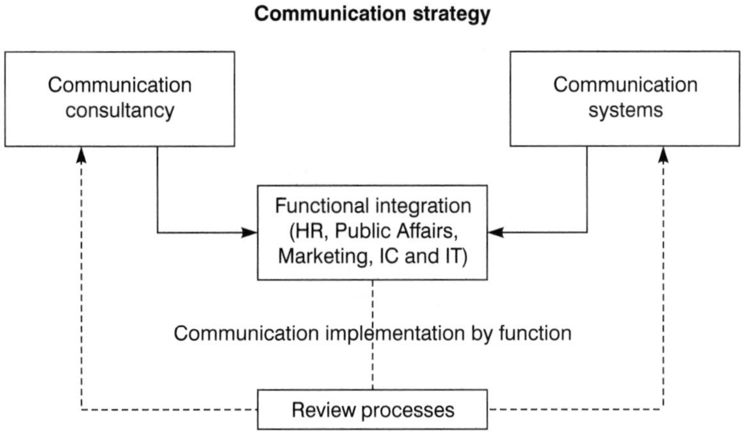

Communication strategy

Figure 11.1 Tomorrow's integrated communication structure

The communication function here has become primarily an internal consultancy, drawing as needed on external expertise, to advise the communication policy and strategy group which is drawn from all the communicating departments. It retains responsibility for maintaining delivery mechanisms, but under the authority of the integrated group. Information technology provides a parallel consultancy and delivery role for communication systems and technologies. A process of constant measurement and review enables communication consultancy and IT to maintain timely, well-founded advice to the communication strategy group.

Planning to become a communicating company

- Convince top management of the value of becoming a communicating company.
- Build alliances/partnerships with other functions, first bilaterally, then across the board.
- Measure when communication failures have cost money/opportunities/employee engagement, and where communication success has made a major contribution.
- Use marketing skills to promote the benefits of effective communication at organization, team and individual levels.
- Apply the principles of communication competence to the communication team, especially as it integrates with the communicating functions.
- Ensure that everyone in the function is clear about its goals and purpose.

- Provide credible leadership and role models for good communication.
- Exemplify the behaviours and processes that lie behind superb information sharing and interface management.
- Benchmark continuously with other IC functions, to acquire better processes and approaches.
- Last, but not least, build your activities and the business case for them around the four pillars of communication in organizations: clarity of business (or project) purpose, trusting interfaces, information sharing and top management communication behaviour!

Summary

This has been a roller-coaster ride through the leading edge of thinking and good practice in internal communication. Our intention has been to open up possibilities, by providing ideas, ammunition and practical starting points for increasing the contribution of employee communication to the performance of organizations. Our research programme continues and will, we expect, provide many more insights into communication excellence in the coming years.

Index